The Improvement Science Dissertation in Practice:

A Guide for Faculty, Committee Members, and their Students

"The authors of this volume are among the pioneers who sought to embed improvement science in the doctoral preparation of educational professionals. In this book, their experience shows. This is not just a book that justifies the use of improvement science tools in the scholarly practice of education. This book shows how those tools can be used to engage in the work of improving educational systems, and how such work can yield a culminating product of learning that demonstrates the rigor required to address real problems in authentic contexts."

Rick McCown, PhD, Professor & Pierre Schouver,
C.S.Sp. Endowed Chair in Mission, Duquesne University

"Once I picked this book up, I couldn't put it down. *The Improvement Science Dissertation in Practice* is a critical read for any university or dissertation committee member wanting to separate from meaningless traditional dissertation practices and instead prepare their EdD candidates to lead and improve complex educational organizations. The book skillfully explicates how the EdD, with an improvement science focus, is rigorous, scientific—and most importantly—supports school leaders in the real-life work of improving their schools and districts. The concepts are riveting, compelling—and practical."

Dr. Deborah S. Peterson, Associate Professor,
Portland State University

"Addressing the needs of the scholar-practitioner doctorate, Perry, Zambo, and Crowe provide an invaluable resource to guide faculty and students' implementation of the Dissertation in Practice. Expanding extensively on improvement science fundamentals that support the teaching and scholarship of the EdD, this important book provides clear principles and guidance for improvement science dissertations in practice that support the journey of all scholarly practitioners."

Elizabeth C. Reilly, Chair & Professor,
Loyola Marymount University

"The tools in this book will help you design a model for rapid personal and organizational change. Our group dissertation in practice took our research beyond the written page and allowed us to apply improvement science to benefit my institution. If you are looking for means to transform educational systems, you've found them."

Brandon Smith, EdD, Associate Dean of Academic Affairs for Student Success, Brevard College

"This work is OUTSTANDING! It is a must read for anyone seeking to understand, redesign, or initiate an Educational Doctorate program in Higher Education. The authors effectively 'demystify' the EdD process in an effort to proactively produce the next generation of educational leaders, change agents if you will, capable of leading change for schools across the educational spectrum. This work is essential for anyone interested in the Educational Doctorate."

Dr. Reginald Wilkerson, Assistant Professor–Clemson University

"Whether we call it improvement science, design-based school improvement, or continuous quality improvement, a logic of organizational development has recently migrated from other industries or fields of work into education that promises to efficiently structure collective improvement efforts and generate new knowledge in partnerships between educational organizations and universities. Doctoral programs in education, leading to an EdD, in which students enmeshed in practice prepare to become strong decision makers and problem solvers at the system level, are a prime site for these partnerships. Here researchers, university-based instructors, and school practitioners meet to jointly develop new knowledge in practice. In this new logic, the EdD dissertation becomes a boundary object between the worlds of university-based research and practice. The book by Perry, Zambo, and Crow does an excellent job in showing the field what faculty and students might need to do to create a dissertation in this new logic. It conceptualizes this type of dissertation by drawing from the knowledge base on professional programs in the field of education; it guides the reader through the essential steps of framing problems, conducting causal analyses, and marshalling the power of change drivers; to end up with a discussion of practical measures that ascertain the success of improvement efforts. The book is a vital source for all those in search for rigorous and practical ways of improving educational organizations and utilizing the education doctorate to get closer to this aim."

Rick Mintrop, Professor, University of California, Berkeley
Author of the book *Design-Based School Improvement*

The
Improvement
Science
Dissertation
in
Practice

THE IMPROVEMENT SCIENCE IN EDUCATION SERIES

Improvement Science (IS) originated in such fields as engineering and health care, but its principal foundation has been found to be an effective school improvement methodology in education. Although improvement science research is so quickly becoming a signature pedagogy and core subject area of inquiry in the field of educational leadership, the literature is still scant in its coverage of IS models. The Improvement Science in Education series is intended to be the most comprehensive collection of volumes to inform educators and researchers about problem analysis, utilization of research, development of solutions, and other practices that can be employed to enhance and strengthen efforts at organizational improvement. This series concentrates on the elements faculty, students, and administrators need to enhance the reliability and validity of improvement or quality enhancement efforts.

BOOKS IN THE SERIES

Editorial submissions

Authors interested in having their manuscripts considered for publication in the Improvement Science in Education Series are encouraged to send a prospectus, sample chapter, and CV to any one of the series editors:
Robert Crow (rcrow@email.wcu.edu),
Brandi Hinnant-Crawford (bnhinnantcrawford@email.wcu.edu), or
Dean T. Spaulding (ds6494@yahoo.com).

The Improvement Science Dissertation in Practice

A Guide for Faculty, Committee Members, and their Students

BY Jill Alexa Perry,
Debby Zambo, and Robert Crow

Myers
Education
Press

Myers
Education
Press

Published by Myers Education Press, LLC
P.O. Box 424
Gorham, ME 04038

Myers Education Press is an academic publisher specializing in books, e-books, and digital content in the field of education. All of our books are subjected to a rigorous peer review process and produced in compliance with the standards of the Council on Library and Information Resources.

Library of Congress Cataloging-in-Publication Data available from Library of Congress.

13-digit ISBN 978-1-9755-0320-8 (paperback)
13-digit ISBN 978-1-9755-0319-2 (hard cover)
13-digit ISBN 978-1-9755-0321-5 (library networkable e-edition)
13-digit ISBN 978-1-9755-0322-2 (consumer e-edition)

Printed in the United States of America.

All first editions printed on acid-free paper that meets the American National Standards Institute Z39-48 standard.

Books published by Myers Education Press may be purchased at special quantity discount rates for groups, workshops, training organizations, and classroom usage. Please call our customer service department at 1-800-232-0223 for details.

Cover and text design by Sophie Appel.

Visit us on the web at **www.myersedpress.com** to browse our complete list of titles.

CONTENTS

DEDICATION

This book is dedicated to EdD students who want skills to change their practice and want their dissertation work to improve their contexts. Your improvement efforts can, and are, solving complex problems of practice. You are scholarly practitioners learning through application, improving education, and generating new knowledge for the stewardship of the profession.

LIST OF FIGURES AND TABLES

Figures

Tables

ACKNOWLEDGEMENTS

We wish to acknowledge ...

Dr. Anthony Bryk, President of the Carnegie Foundation for the Advancement of Teaching, for leading the members of Carnegie Project on the Education Doctorate (CPED) down the improvement path. Without his prompting, the authors of this book would not have begun to make the links between improvement science and the dissertation in practice.

The many team members of the Carnegie Foundation who taught us improvement science and supported our ideas about making it a signature methodology for the education doctorate.

Dr. Rick Mintrop who inspired us to move his work on design-based improvement forward and who has been a thought partner in this work.

The faculty and deans of CPED member institutions who were early adopters of improvement science and learned by doing while teaching it to their scholarly practitioners.

Brandi Nicole Hinnant-Crawford, Robert Crow, and Dean T. Spaulding for accepting this volume into their edited series.

Emma Abruzzo who patiently edited this volume for us.

Each of our families who offered us patience and support.

FOREWORD

We continue to witness how rapid demographic and technological changes place increasing pressure on districts and schools. Across the country, school leaders are being asked to shift their work away from serving as managers of schools towards leaders of learning organizations. School boards are asking superintendents to create schools where teachers hone their practice within learning communities and encourage children to collaborate with their peers. At the same time, superintendents are turning to schools of education and demanding them to prepare more leaders capable of working in these new ways. Yet, more often than not, school districts struggle to establish organizations that are top-to-bottom learning communities, and schools of education have yet to figure out how to reliably produce leaders with the knowledge, skills, and disposition necessary to build and lead learning communities where children, regardless of who they are or where they come from, have equal opportunities and outcomes.

These challenges have encouraged us to look to improvement science as a way to make progress. With its roots in management theory, improvement science employs disciplined inquiry to solve persistent problems of practice. Improvement science bloomed in healthcare during the 1990s and has spread rapidly to other sectors, including education. This is, in part, due to the work of the Carnegie Foundation for the Advancement of Teaching. We see in these growing pressures on our schools the need to ensure that the discipline, methods, and tools of continuous improvement play a central role in the methodological and conceptual preparation of next-generation leaders.

As improvement ideas have spread, a growing number of colleges and universities have begun integrating improvement science as a key component of their leadership programs and offerings, including creating new modules and courses of study and redesigning capstone and culminating projects. Moreover, many postsecondary institutions are partnering with community districts and schools to create networked improvement communities to use improvement science to solve thorny and local educational problems and provide their graduate students with meaningful, hands-on improvement experiences.

Given these developments, this volume provides timely and valuable guidance for faculty, students, and practitioners seeking to pursue practical and scholarly work in educational improvement. For EdD programs, improvement science provides a promising vehicle to transform the current dissertation in practice into a different testimony of candidate proficiency and know-how. The authors provide us with critical context and history about the professional practice doctorate, including the recent efforts of over 100 postsecondary institutions in the Carnegie Project on the Education Doctorate to revitalize the EdD to focus on the development of leaders who tackle issues of equity and social justice and who are able to partner with others to fundamentally transform schools and other learning organizations. Further, and nearly at every turn, these authors push us to reflect on the kinds of attitudes and competencies we will need and want from our leaders to effectively change entrenched systems that continue to privilege some children while depriving others of essential opportunities.

Studies consistently indicate that leadership matters for the well-being of students and schools. While reforms in preparation programs have sought to better train leaders to attend to context-specific conditions and dynamics, they remain largely disconnected from the communities they serve and the problems that confront them. Improvement science can provide this bridging mechanism and a more practical means to cultivate leaders who will persist in dismantling stubborn inequities and forge forward in problem-focused, student-centered, hopeful ways.

Manuelito Biag, PhD
Senior Associate, Networked Improvement Science
Carnegie Foundation for the Advancement of Teaching

CHAPTER ONE

Designing a Professional Practice Doctorate

From the beginning of the Carnegie Project on the Education Doctorate (CPED) in 2007, the most questioned component of EdD program redesign has been the culminating research project. The CPED consortium began with the idea of a "capstone," but it was unsure of what that meant. Members debated the name. Capstone sounded too much like undergraduate work. The term seemed to diminish the importance of a doctorate. Members suggested sticking with the term "dissertation," but they then grappled with the question: *How is an EdD dissertation different than a PhD dissertation?* In those early years, CPED faculty members were unsure of what the final product should be called or what it should look like. They could, however, agree on some central tenants of this culminating product: the major focus should be problems of practice, the research should be applied, and development of the product should be built throughout and across the coursework. With these tenants, CPED faculty members set off to distinguish the EdD capstone from the PhD dissertation.

The work to distinguish the capstone from the dissertation produced various models—thematic dissertations, action research projects, case studies, and group or team evaluation products— that played out in different contexts with different kinds of student practitioners. Members spent bi-annual CPED convening time actively discussing the purpose of this experience, the ways to assess it, and if it was needed at all. In fact, in 2014, Joe Murphy of Peabody College of Education and Human Development at Vanderbilt University challenged CPED faculty to consider eliminating the dissertation/culminating product altogether. He argued that it served no purpose in preparing leaders to change practice. Yet, despite not quite knowing what the answer should be, members pushed back and agreed that a dissertation was both necessary and important in EdD programs.

The EdD and the Dissertation

According to the Council of Graduate Schools' (CGS) *Task Force Report on the Professional Doctorate* (2007), professional doctorates fall into two categories: those with a dissertation and those without. The degrees that have a dissertation have "no direct relationship to licensure and have a significant relationship to clinical, translational, or engaged research" (p. 12). Because the field of education does not have a licensure body, some product or experience is needed to demonstrate to the faculty that the student is qualified and has done the work worthy of earning the education doctorate degree. Colwill (2012) has termed any professional degree that requires a dissertation as a *Professional Research Doctorate*, one that focuses on both research and practice and that requires a dissertation to "investigate a particular professional topic or existing problem" (p. 13). CPED members have strived to reframe the dissertation in their EdD programs to make them align with Colwill's definition. This task, however, has not been simple for a variety of reasons.

First, historically, the dissertation is synonymous with doctoral education. The idea stems from the German university Doctor of Philosophy model, or PhD, that was adopted in the United States in the late 1800s. The PhD had a significant research component, and preparation for this degree was meant "to confer expertise by winnowing out the amateurs from the experts" which was done through the writing of an "elaborate thesis ... a rigorous test of intellectual mettle" (Loss, 2015, p. 3) known as the dissertation. At the end of the nineteenth century, the professions of law and medicine sought to adopt a similar credentialing model to demonstrate an individual's professional competence. Education followed suit by entering the academy and seeking to establish itself as a profession with a doctoral degree. Teachers College, Columbia University created the first PhD in Education in 1893, which was aimed at preparing school administrative professionals. Harvard College also sought to prepare administrative professionals but wanted a different degree title and created the Education Doctorate, or EdD, in 1920. Unlike law and medicine, however, the training in these new doctorates in education were very much modeled after the Doctor of Philosophy which traditionally was awarded by the graduate school of arts and sciences. To distinguish the EdD from the PhD, coursework was reduced, and dissertations emphasized research on technical problems rather than research for knowledge generation. Though the goal was noble, rather than solidify the profession of education, these early actions merely confused the two degrees and caused the EdD to be viewed as the lesser of the two degrees. Consequently, the professional practice of education never gained the respect that other professions, like medicine and law, have.

Second, most educational faculty are not prepared to design EdD programs and don't always know what practitioners need. Holding a PhD in Education does not require that one has had practitioner experience, nor do PhD programs teach prospective faculty members how to design preparation programs for practitioners. As a result, faculty members in schools of education have tended to prepare practitioners as they were prepared in their own PhD programs but with less strict requirements and lower expectations for the research generated by these practitioners. Over time, the confusing beginnings of the EdD combined with weak program designs diminished the value of the EdD.

Third, for educational practitioners who have sought a doctorate (whether it was an EdD or PhD), the dissertation experience and product have generally been viewed as a hoop-jumping exercise. Even though the investigative work of the dissertation provided information and learning, it rarely resulted in skills to advance careers (beyond a credential) or to improve one's ability to impact the problems faced daily (Mehta, Gomez, & Bryk, 2011; Perry, 2013). Programs have neglected the fact that practitioners are a different kind of student with different kinds of needs. In general, those who seek a doctorate are "experienced practitioners" (Tupling & Outhwaite, 2017, p. 154) that are older and generally have between 10 and 20 years of professional experience. Many are highly qualified, successful leaders who carry an immense amount of professional expertise into their program of study (Perry, 2013; Willis, Inman, & Valenti, 2010). Additionally, these students want to remain on their career trajectory and look for part-time programs to earn their degree while they continue to work. This type of student presents the "inverse of other fields" (Shulman, Golde, Beuschel, & Garabedian, 2006, p. 26), which generally sees younger students who continue from their undergraduate program through to their doctorate without having spent time working in a professional field.

Furthermore, in many cases, these educational practitioners face the dilemma of needing to obtain a doctorate to advance in their careers but encounter doctoral preparation that isn't suited to their professional needs. They enter doctoral study eager to gain stronger skills and abilities that will help them address the pressing issues they face in their daily practice. Frequently, however, the only program options are traditional doctoral programs that don't necessarily offer practical skills, nor do they offer the knowledge of how to apply theory and research to practice. These practitioners sacrifice time away from work and family, spending hard-earned money (part-time students do not qualify for financial aid) to obtain a degree that does not support their professional development beyond credentialing. As students in traditional programs, they write dissertations that are theoretically based and struggle to apply the experience and knowledge to their practice settings. The dissertation experience is very different from what students in other professions find. Often professional training in other fields teaches methods and acumen that are contextualized in applied, experiential, and utilization-focused ways of practice. For instance, medical students work in hospitals alongside licensed doctors to learn diagnosing skills and behavioral interventions. Surgeons learn to sew as part of their curriculum and practice over and over. Lawyers practice arguing and debating through the Socratic method that teaches them necessary critical thinking. Clergy learn to console. Engineers practice methods of design. In contrast, educational doctoral students who seek to remain in practice typically received no such hands-on training. Rarely have traditional programs provided practical application of theory to practice. The end result of such preparation was a credential that supported career advancement but offered little in the way of useful skills to help practitioners improve the practice of education (Perry, 2012a).

When the Carnegie Foundation for the Advancement of Teaching offered funds in 2007 to create a consortium that would undertake the examination of the EdD, it did so at a crucial point in U.S. educational history. Years of educational reforms, calls for accountability, and pressure from inside and outside of schools of education to improve the way practitioners were prepared made the EdD an apt target. Lee Shulman, then-president of the Carnegie Foundation, and his colleagues spent the five years prior to this initiative examining signature pedagogies in PhD and professional preparation programs across several fields. Education was the only field that crossed both projects that prepared researchers and professionals. They concluded with a call to schools of education to clearly define both the EdD and PhD degrees or "risk becoming increasingly impotent in carrying out their primary missions—the advancement of knowledge and the preparation of quality practitioners" (Shulman et al., 2006, p. 25). CPED was created as a result. Faculty from 25 schools of education were tasked to clarify and define the EdD as the professional practice doctorate in education. Though a seemingly easy task, members found early on that a one-size-fits-all model would not work in education as it had in medicine, engineering, and other professional fields. The profession of education spans PK-12 schooling, post-secondary education, out-of-school learning, non-profit leadership, and beyond. Attempts to create one EdD program design failed as members realized not all educational practitioners needed the same kind of preparation. For example, a superintendent in Houston could not be prepared in the same way as a community college leader in rural Kentucky because their needs and contexts were so vastly different. What emerged was groundbreaking. Members suggested that a set of principles could offer guidance but remain flexible enough to accommodate various types of programs, practitioner needs, and local university regulations. Over two convenings in 2009, original CPED faculty members pooled together the defined outcomes for their programs and worked collaboratively to develop the CPED Guiding Principles and a new definition of the Education Doctorate. Combined with the design concepts that were developed over the first three years of the project, CPED members created a framework to guide the design of professional practice doctoral programs and to reestablish the EdD as the professional doctorate in education.

Beginning with the End

The CGS *Task Force Report on the Professional Doctorate* (2007) states the professional doctorate should prepare someone for "the potential transformation of that field of professional practice, just as the PhD represents preparation for the potential transformation of the basic knowledge in a discipline" (p. 6). Seeking to apply the Task Force's conclusion to the EdD, CPED members developed the following definition: "The professional doctorate in education prepares educators for the application of appropriate and specific practices, the generation of new knowledge, and for the stewardship of the profession" (CPED, 2010). This new definition requires that EdD program are not designed by subtraction of requirements but rather are redesigned around the needs of the profession. Such program redesign requires two components. First, faculty must define the skills, knowledge, and habits that a graduate will have as a result of attending the program. Second, faculty must create a cohesive program design where components and assessments build upon each other to ensure the graduate earns the defined skills, knowledge, and habits.

Defining the graduate

When designing an EdD program, it is essential that faculty begin with the end goal in mind. Asking, "Who do we want to graduate as a result of this program?" can guide faculty in understanding what skills they want students to gain, what core knowledge they need, and what character traits they should hold as a result of the program. This question requires that faculty understand who students of these programs are, knowing what skills, knowledge, and expertise they bring with them to the program, and how they as their teachers will enhance and build upon that existing expertise. Understanding how to take an already highly qualified practitioner and providing them with the skills and abilities to transform practice can be time consuming and unfamiliar for many faculty (Perry, 2013). In contrast, shifting around courses, subtracting credit hours, or reducing content in research courses may seem more familiar and quicker. However, resorting to this kind of program redesign can reinforce the notion of the EdD as PhD-lite. Rather, faculty need to consider (through data gathering, focus groups, and market analysis) what the practitioners with whom they work need to become better (Gawande, 2007). Such professional needs, when combined with faculty areas of expertise, can shape a strong program that supports the defined graduate outcomes.

Consider that the dimensions of professional preparation in education can also help shape graduate outcomes. In 1986, Stark, Lowther, and Hagerty outlined two dimensions of professional preparation—building *competencies* and fostering *attitudes*—that may be useful in thinking about the skills, knowledge, and habits an EdD graduate should have. The professional competencies and attitudes are described in the table below. Note Table 1.1.

As a start to program redesign, these competencies and attitudes can provide discussion points about who the specific EdD program is looking to graduate. Program faculty will also want to conduct a local needs assessment, determine their institution's rules and regulations that govern graduate education, and determine who potential students might be.

Table 1.1. Professional Competencies & Attitudes (Stark et al., 1986)

Professional Competencies	Professional Attitudes
Conceptual: possessing theoretical understanding	**Career marketability:** the degree to which the graduate is employable
Technical: the ability to perform tasks	**Professional identity:** the degree to which the graduate internalizes norms of the profession
Contextual: the understanding of work environments	**Ethical standards:** the degree to which the graduate internalizes the ethics of a profession
Interpersonal communication: the ability to communicate effectively in writing and orally	**Scholarly concern for improvement:** the degree to which the graduate recognizes the need to increase knowledge of the profession through research
Integrative: the ability to combine theory and technical skills into practice	**Motivation for continued learning:** the degree to which the graduate seeks to update knowledge and skills
Adaptive skills: the ability to anticipate and accommodate change in the profession	

Ideally the design concepts found in the CPED Framework can guide these discussions. The seven design concepts are Scholarly Practitioner, Signature Pedagogy, Laboratory of Practice, Inquiry as Practice, Mentoring and Advising, Problem of Practice (PoP), and Dissertation in Practice (DiP) (see www.cpedinitiative.org/the-framework for definitions). An example of how these design concepts guide a program design is the Scholarly Practitioner, or the graduate of a CPED-influenced EdD program. CPED defines this graduate as someone who can:

> blend practical wisdom with professional skills and knowledge to name, frame, and solve problems of practice; use practical research and applied theories as tools for change because they understand the importance of equity and social justice; disseminate their work in multiple ways, and have an obligation to resolve problems of

practice by collaborating with key stakeholders, including the university, the educational institution, the community, and individuals. (CPED, 2010)

The definition of the scholarly practitioner offers faculty members language to build into their graduate outcomes such as applying theory in practical settings and understanding how to design and do applied research as leadership tools for change. Throughout this book, we refer to students of EdD program as Scholarly Practitioners to support our ideas of applying improvement science to the DiP.

Another example of applying a design concept is inquiry as practice. Whereas in the past, the EdD was defined by subtraction of research credits and weaker dissertation designs, the scholarly practitioner definition calls for the amplification of research preparation. CPED terms this skill as *inquiry as practice*, or the

> process of posing significant questions that focus on complex problems of practice. By using various research, theories, and professional wisdom, scholarly practitioners design innovative solutions to address the problems of practice. At the center of inquiry of practice is the ability to use data to understand the effects of innovation. As such, inquiry of practice requires the ability to gather, organize, judge, aggregate, and analyze situations, literature, and data with a critical lens. (CPED, 2010)

This definition offers enhanced skills, knowledge, and habits that can further aid faculty in defining EdD graduate outcomes. Golde (2013) explains how scholarly practitioners utilize inquiry as practice. She says they

> learn to see important questions in the world of practice, frame those questions in terms of rigorous inquiry, answer those questions by generating and analyzing data, share what they have learned with other stakeholders, and directly apply what they have learned in settings of practice. (p. 145)

Building a cohesive program

Once faculty have created a set of graduate outcomes, they can backward map their program from these outcomes. Backward mapping is a deliberate, informed, contextual process that focuses on programmatic outcomes (Thomson et al., 2017; Wiggins & McTighe, 2005). The backward mapping process "systematically maps a clear pathway to specific and explicit learning goals, positioning a range of experiences and opportunities along the pathway to support learners to successfully complete assessment tasks that demonstrate achievement of the goals" (Thomson et al., 2017, p. 360). Starting with the graduate outcomes and working their way backwards, faculty redesign the program components (e.g., assessments, coursework, activities and even admissions processes) that lead to these outcomes. This process will ensure that the practitioner who was admitted to the program builds upon their existing abilities to gain the competencies and attitudes identified by the faculty to improve their educational practice. The first of these components is the dissertation. CPED members intentionally chose the term *dissertation in practice* to maintain the notion of conferring expertise upon a graduate who had completed a rigorous process while also distinguishing the EdD culminating product from the PhD dissertation. A DiP is defined as a "scholarly endeavor that impacts a complex problem of practice" (CPED, 2010). It is meant to prepare "students for the type of post graduate work they will be doing" (Sugimoto, 2015, p. 2).

Additional program components can be supported by the Guiding Principles of Program Design found in the CPED Framework which offer a foundation upon which to build the program. The principles state that an EdD program:

1. is framed around questions of equity, ethics, and social justice to bring about solutions to complex problems of practice;
2. prepares leaders who can construct and apply knowledge to make a positive difference in the lives of individuals, families, organizations, and communities;
3. provides opportunities for candidates to develop and demon-

strate collaboration and communication skills to work with diverse communities and to build partnerships;

4. provides field-based opportunities to analyze problems of practice and use multiple frames to develop meaningful solutions;

5. is grounded in and develops a professional knowledge base that
integrates both practical and research knowledge, that links
theory with systemic and systematic inquiry; and

6. emphasizes the generation, transformation, and use of professional knowledge and practice.

CPED member institutions have utilized these principles to re/
design and evaluate their programs. In the design process, as faculty
backward map from the graduate outcomes, the principles inform
development of programmatic components such as core courses,
inquiry courses, content area courses, experiential learning exercises, and assessments. These components are where students
learn the skills, knowledge, and habits that they will demonstrate in
their DiP. The CPED design concepts then offer building blocks to
support the development of these program components. The design
concepts are listed in the below table. Note Table 1.2.

The design concepts are the "how" of program design. Through
signature pedagogies and tailored mentoring and advising, faculty
guide practitioners by means of professional learning. Through
problems of practice and inquiry as practice, students learn to

Table 1.2. CPED Design Concept Definitions

Scholarly Practitioner	blends practical wisdom with professional skills and knowledge to name, frame, and solve problems of prac-tice; uses practical research and applied theories as tools for change because they understand the importance of equity and social justice; disseminates their work in multiple ways; resolves PoPs by collaborating with key stakeholders including the university, the educational institution, the community, and individuals.
Signature Pedagogy	the pervasive set of practices used to prepare scholarly practitioners for all aspects of their professional work: "to think, to perform, and to act with integrity" (Shul-man, 2005, p. 52).

Laboratories of Practice	settings where theory and practice inform and enrich each other. They address complex PoPs where ideas—formed by the intersection of theory, inquiry, and practice—can be implemented, measured, and analyzed for the impact made. Laboratories of Practice facilitate transformative and generative learning that is measured by the development of scholarly expertise and implementation of practice.
Problem of Practice	a persistent, contextualized, and specific issue embedded in the work of a professional practitioner, the addressing of which has the potential to result in improved understanding, experience, and outcomes.
Inquiry as Practice	the process of posing significant questions that focus on complex PoPs, the ability to use data to understand the effects of innovation, and the ability to gather, organize, judge, aggregate, and analyze situations, literature, and data with a critical lens.
Dissertation in Practice	a scholarly endeavor that impacts a complex PoP.
Mentoring & Advising	guided by: equity and justice, mutual respect, dynamic learning, flexibility, intellectual space, and supportive and safe learning environments; centralizes students' needs and PoPs in learning; expects rigorous practices; aligns with adult learner needs while reflecting a program's values, norms, and the CPED Framework.

systematically identify problems in their professional settings and how to investigate and test solutions for solving them using research methodologies and gathering empirical evidence. Finally, through laboratories of practice, students gain hands-on experience in being a scholarly practitioner.

Whether or not the CPED Framework is utilized in designing an EdD program, the central point of backward mapping (Thomson et al., 2017) is the building of a cohesive program whereby the learning from each component is scaffolded upon the component that comes before it. The components work together to facilitate student proficiency with the skills, knowledge, and habits described in the graduate outcomes. Note Figure 1.1, which displays the backward mapping process.

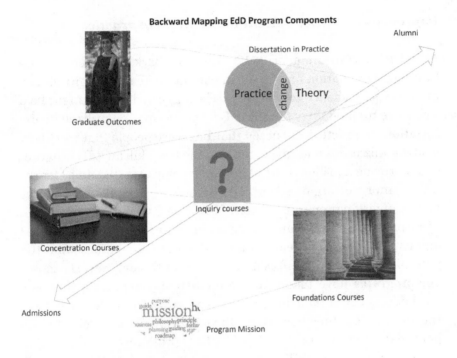

Figure 1.1. EdD Program Backward Mapping Process

The DiP will serve as the culminating activity that demonstrates the student has the expertise described in the program's graduate outcomes allowing the faculty to confer the degree. In many CPED programs, the chosen signature pedagogy is the DiP and how it is embedded into the program components. This process often starts in the first semester with the definition of a *problem of practice*. Students home in on this problem through the application of literature to better define the problem by considering how to apply inquiry to improve the problem and finally implementing an inquiry process. All of this takes place during the course work and laboratories. Embedding the dissertation process across the program gives students and faculty the opportunity to work together as learning occurs and to centralize the student and their practice in the program.

Improvement science and the dissertation in practice

At a CPED convening in 2012, Anthony Bryk, president of the Carnegie Foundation for the Advancement of Teaching, introduced improvement science to members. He suggested that it might be a signature methodology taught in EdD programs and utilized in dissertations in practice. He noted that EdDs are people that will likely lead organizations and suggested that the best skill an EdD program could provide a leader is the ability to develop and sustain a "learning to improve" organization. Dr. Bryk further challenged members to envision preparing teams of improvers who might tackle the same problem across many educational contexts. As a result, CPED and its members have learned alongside the Foundation about the potential of improvement science for practitioners. Several member programs have taken up the challenge, integrating this new methodology into their programs. As members have learned from the Foundation, they have come to view improvement science as a potential signature methodology for EdD programs.

The authors of this text see synergy between the Carnegie Foundation's Six Core Principles of Improvement and the CPED Guiding Principles for Program Design. Both sets seek to give a new and different way of "doing" to educational practitioners. Note Table 1.3, where we offer a comparison.

In *The Educational Leader's Guide to Improvement Science: Data, Design and Cases for Reflection (Improvement Science in Education and Beyond)* (Crow, Hinnant-Crawford, & Spaulding, 2019), Perry, Crow, and Zambo (2019) argue that improvement science offers a "promising means" (p. 147) for preparing scholarly practitioners to apply inquiry as a tool for improving problems of practice. We distinguish research *for* practice from research *on* practice to emphasize that practitioners are insiders who are closest to the problem and have the means to articulate the problem, understand the variability, and perform rapid tests of change that will help them to "learn fast and implement [change] well" (Perry, Crow, & Zambo, 2019, p. 158). Improvement science offers a valuable set of tools with distinct skills, knowledge, and habits that can support leaders in improving their systems and organizations.

Table 1.3. Comparison of CPED Guiding Principles for Program Design & the Carnegie Foundation's Six Core Principles of Improvement

CPED's Guiding Principles for Program Design	The Six Core Principles of Improvement
The professional doctorate in education: 1. is framed around questions of equity, ethics, and social justice to bring about solutions to complex problems of practice. *Students are taught to incorporate an equity and justice lens as they understand problems and systems. They pose solutions that bring about equitable change in an ethical manner.*	1. Make the work problem-specific and user-centered. *It starts with a single question: "What specifically is the problem we are trying to solve?" It enlivens a co-development orientation: engage key participants early and often.*
2. prepares leaders who can construct and apply knowledge to make a positive difference in the lives of individuals, families, organizations, and communities. *Theoretical knowledge is taught as a tool for changing those people and communities that the leaders serves.*	2. Variation in performance is the core problem to address. *The critical issue is not what works, but rather what works, for whom, and under what set of conditions. Aim to advance efficacy reliably at scale.*
3. provides opportunities for candidates to develop and demonstrate collaboration and communication skills to work with diverse communities and to build partnerships. *Opportunities for engaging and speaking multiple people and communities to learn with and for them through partnerships that bring about positive change.*	3. See the system that produces the current outcomes. *It is hard to improve what you do not fully understand. Go and see* how local conditions shape work processes. *Make your* hypotheses *for change public and clear.*
4. provides field-based opportunities to analyze PoPs and use multiple frames to develop meaningful solutions. *Gives students hands-on activities that allows them to practice identifying problems through theoretical and practices lenses.*	4. We cannot improve at scale what we cannot measure. *Embed measures of key outcomes and processes to track if change is an improvement. We intervene in complex organizations. Anticipate unintended consequences and measure these too.*
5. is grounded in and develops a professional knowledge base that integrates both practical and research knowledge, that links theory with systemic and systematic inquiry. *Respects and honors practitioner knowledge and teaches tools to integrate literature in furthering understanding of systems as roots of problems.*	5. Anchor practice improvement in disciplined inquiry. *Engage rapid cycles of plan, do, study, act (PDSA) to learn fast, fail fast, and improve quickly. That failures may occur is not the problem; that we fail to learn from them is.*
6. emphasizes the generation, transformation, and use of professional knowledge and practice. *As scholarly practitioners, graduates become Stewards of the Profession.*	6. Accelerate improvements through networked communities. *Embrace the wisdom of crowds. We can accomplish more together than even the best of us can accomplish alone.*

Arguments have been made for why improvement science is needed in education. Such arguments point to the fact that past efforts of applying research and development to education have taken too long, have rarely incorporated those who are engaged in education on a daily basis, and have produced little change (Bryk, 2015; Donovan, 2013; Lewis, 2015). If our goal in redesigning the EdD is to better prepare practitioners to address the problems they face, then we have to give them the skills, knowledge, and habits to do so. Improvement science can fill this need.

As students learn the skills and knowledge of improvement science, they will develop the habits of an *improver*. Lucas and Nacer (2015) have defined these habits in healthcare, which can align with most any profession with the primary purpose of serving others, like education. Note Figure 1.2 of these habits.

Figure 1.2. Habits of an Improver (Lucas & Nacer, 2015)

The habits of the improver align with both the CPED Framework and the Six Core Principles of Improvement. The habits also fit the definition of a profession as described by Shulman (2007). In his address at the CGS annual meeting, Shulman (2007) argued the need to make the EdD *the* professional degree in education. He defined and described a profession as one that:

1. provides a service to society;
2. is performed in exchange for autonomy;
3. possesses a growing body of knowledge, research, and practice;
4. possesses a mastery of technical skills and practices;
5. holds the ability to make judgments under uncertainty;
6. holds the ability to learn from experience, error, and others; and
7. has a professional community that sets standards, monitors quality, and offers continued education and development.

If a secondary goal of redesigning the EdD is to distinguish it as a professional degree, then aligning it with improvement science and the habits that practitioners develop makes sense. In doing so, faculty have the opportunity to render schools of education more relevant and more accountable than they have been. But first, faculty members must be improvers. They must see themselves not only as researchers but also as preparers of professional practitioners and as teachers of improvement. They must hold themselves accountable for creating strong, practitioner-focused EdD programs and for developing assessments that ensure practitioners learn the skills, knowledge, and habits they need. Backward mapping a program design and developing an Improvement Science Dissertation in Practice (ISDiP) are ways to deliver on these demands. A true learning institution values innovation and the free exchange of ideas and engages in continuous improvement activities to enhance both student and faculty experiences.

What's to Come

As a guide, this book builds on the above ideas. Each chapter offers reflective questions, illustrations, or examples that will support faculty who wish to use improvement science as a signature methodology and guide students through the dissertation process at a deeper, more complex level. The book will support students wanting to write an ISDiP that makes real differences on the pressing problems they face. Additionally, the text will assist committee members mentoring students through this new dissertation process. We invite you to engage with the following chapters to learn more.

Summary

In this chapter, we have provided some background and history about the dissertation and doctoral education. We have argued for the distinction of the dissertation in EdD programs and provided a means, backward mapping, for making the EdD dissertation more relevant in program design. We noted that the CPED Principles for Program Design align with the Carnegie Foundation for the Advancement of Teaching's Six Core Principles of Improvement, which creates a foundation upon which to bring improvement science into EdD programs. We also introduced the notion of applying improvement science to the DiP by suggesting that improvement science might be a signature methodology for better preparing practitioners to address the pressing problems they face in their practice.

Post-reading questions for faculty

1. Utilizing the dimensions of competencies and attitudes, what are the skills, knowledge, and dispositions that define your EdD program's graduate outcomes?
2. What aspects of your program prepare Scholarly Practitioners?

Post-reading questions for Scholarly Practitioners/Students

1. Examine your thinking about a dissertation. What have been your expectations? How have those aligned or not with your program?
2. What are your goals for your dissertation?
3. How do you envision becoming a scholarly practitioner will support your professional practice?

References

Bryk, A.S. (2015). Accelerating how we learn to improve, *Educational Researcher, 44*(9), 467–477.

Bryk, A.S., Gomez, L.M., Gunrow, A., & LeMahieu, P.G. (2017). *Learning to improve: How America's schools can get better at getting better.* Cambridge, MA, Harvard Education Press.

Carnegie Project for the Educational Doctorate (CPED). (2009). *Working principles for the professional practice doctorate in education.* Retrieved from http://cpedinitiative.org

Carnegie Project for the Educational Doctorate (CPED). (2010). *Design concept definitions.* Retrieved from http://cpedinitiative.org

Colwill, D.A. (2012). *Educating the scholar practitioner in organization development (Contemporary Trends in Organization Development and Change).* Charlotte, NC: Information Age.

Council of Graduate Schools (2007). *Task force report on the professional doctorate.* Washington, DC.

Crow, R., Hinnant-Crawford, B.N., & Spaulding, D.T. (Eds.). (2019). *The educational leader's guide to improvement science: Data, design and cases for reflection.* Gorham, Maine: Myers Education Press.

Donovan, M.S. (2013). Generating improvement through research and development in educations systems. *Science. 340*(6130). pp. 317–319.

Gawande, A. (2007). *Better: A surgeon's notes on performance.* New York: Metropolitan Books.

Golde, C. (2013). Afterword: Mapping the transformation of the Ed.D. student. In Perry, J.A. & Carlson, D.L., (Eds.). *In their own words: A journey to the stewardship of the practice in education.* Charlotte, NC: Information Age Publishing.

Lewis, C. (2015). What is improvement science? Do we need it in education? *Educational Researcher, 44*(1), pp. 54–61.

Loss, C. (2016). Future of the dissertation: A brief history of doctoral discourse. proceedings from the Council of Graduate Schools' what is a doctorate? Online Proceedings of the 2016 Global Summit.

Lucas, B. & Nacer, H. (2015). The habits of an improver: Thinking about learning for improvement in health care. London: Health Foundation.

Mehta, J.D., Gomez, L.M., Bryk, A.S. (2011). Schooling as a knowledge profession. *Education Week.* 30(26), p. 27.

Perry, J.A. (2012). To EdD or not to EdD? *Phi Delta Kappan. 94*(1), pp. 41–44.

Perry, J.A. (2013). Developing stewards of practice. In Perry, J.A. & Carlson, D.L. (Eds.). (2013). *In their own words: A journey to the stewardship of the practice in education.* Charlotte, NC: Information Age Publishing.

Perry, J.A. & Zambo, D. (2019). Developing stewards of the practice: Understanding the role of improvement science. In Crow, R., Hinnant-Crawford, B. N., & Spaulding, D. T. (Eds.). (2019). *The educational leader's guide to improvement science: Data, design and cases for reflection.* Gorham, Maine: Myers Education Press.

Shulman, L.S. (2005). Signature pedagogies in the professions. *Daedalus, 134*(3), 52–59.

Shulman, L.S. (2007). *Scholarships of practice and the practice of scholarship: Education among the doctorates.* Paper presented at the Council of Graduate Schools.

Shulman, L.S., Golde, C.M., Bueschel, A.C., & Garabedian, K.J. (2006). Reclaiming education's doctorates: A critique and a proposal. *Educational Researcher, 35*(3), 25–32.

Stark, J.S., Lowther, M.A., & Hagerty, B.M.K. (1986). *Responsive professional education: Balancing outcomes and opportunities.* Washington, DC: The George Washington University.

Sugimoto, C.R. (2015). Toward a twenty-first century dissertation. Proceedings from the Council of Graduate Schools' What Is a Doctorate? Online Proceedings of the 2016 Global Summit.

Thomson, E.A., Auhl, G., Hicks, K., McPherson, K., Robinson, C., & Wood, D. (2017). Course design as a collaborative enterprise: Incorporating interdisciplinarity into a backward mapping systems approach to course design in Higher Education. In R. Walker, & S. Bedford (Eds.), *Research and development in higher education: Curriculum transformation volume 40: Refereed papers from the 40th HERDSA Annual International Conference* (pp. 356–367). [Paper 85] Sydney, NSW: Higher Education Research and Development Society of Australasia.

Tupling, C. & Outhwaite, D. (2017). *Developing an identity as an Ed.D leader: a reflexive narrative account. Management in Education, 31*(4). pp. 153–158.

Wiggins, G., & McTighe, J. (2005). *Understanding by design.* Ascd.

Willis, J.W., Inman, D., & Valenti, R. (2010). *Completing a professional practice dissertation: A guide for doctoral students and faculty*. Charlotte, NC: Information Age Publishing.

CHAPTER TWO

New Mindsets and a New Dissertation Frame

Building on the idea of developing scholarly practitioners with Dissertations in Practice (DiPs) using an improvement science frame, this chapter will a) provide a rationale for educational translational researchers; b) explain why improvement science is a science; c) explain the distinction between a DiP and a traditional 5-chapter dissertation; and d) present a new framework for an Improvement Science Dissertation in Practice (ISDiP).

If you are a student in an EdD program, you may know someone who has successfully written and defended their dissertation and you expect to do the same. You expect to be successful by working in isolation and putting in many hours and resources. It is also likely that you want your dissertation to matter, to not sit on a shelf collecting dust as so many do. As a working professional, you want your work to make a difference, to spread, and to be useful to others and yourself. As a doctoral student, you want to make it through graduate school, but you know that not all students who start a program finish. It is likely you know, or will come to know, a few ABD (All But Dissertation) students, those students who completed all of their coursework but never finished their dissertation. In education, attrition from doctoral programs is estimated at approximately 50%. In addition, about 20% of these give up at the dissertation stage (Bowen & Rudenstine, 1992; Cesari, 1990).

If you are a faculty or committee member, it is likely that you have successfully written and defended your dissertation. You may recall the stress of trying to find a researchable topic (linked to your major professor's area of interest), writing an exhaustive literature review that situated your topic within the literature or filled a gap, securing a site to collect data, recruiting participants, setting out to gather data over several months, and then analyzing the data you collected in isolation. Your work likely produced deep knowledge about your topic in a specific domain and, given your position, it is likely that this served you well. Work from your dissertation probably became the start of your academic career and publication record. Your dissertation was likely a ritual object in a complex rite of passage developed to anoint a priesthood of scholars like yourself (Willis, Valenti, & Inman, 2010). The mental map you have of writing and defending your dissertation is one of pride and struggle. It contains all the good and bad emotions you experienced during the process. It is also likely that these positive and negative experiences will influence how you work with your students. Having received a PhD, you expect your students to be proud of their work, to work efficiently and individually. You expect a well-written, 5-chapter product that will in turn lead your own students to a faculty position and a publication record of their own.

As you read this chapter, be aware that students, faculty, and committee members come to the dissertation process with varied experiences, emotions, and expectations. This chapter will make you more aware of your own views and, hopefully, open your mind to the idea that dissertation work and products in EdD programs should both provide practical, applicable skills to practitioners and be useful and impactful. No matter who you are, this chapter will help you develop a new mindset around dissertations and the EdD.

New Mindsets: Translational Researchers

Dissertations can be mysterious, challenging, and the point in a doctoral program where students fall down. We contend that the dissertation experience does not have to be so complicated. For EdD students in particular, dissertation work can be productive (and even exciting) if it crosses the theory-to-practice divide. The right kind of dissertation work can improve contexts, develop thoughtful leaders, and expand professional knowledge that is useful to others. To accomplish these goals, we need to think about developing both the kind of individuals who can do this work and the type of training and culminating project they need. Educational research, including the research in dissertations, has not always been helpful in the practice arena. Over the years, many calls for change have been made. For example, Clandinin and Connelly (1995) argued that the propositional and theoretical knowledge from research that filters into practice has little appreciation for the personal, subjective, historical, and relational patterns that exist there. Likewise, in her 2012 presidential address to the American Educational Research Association, Arnetha Ball (2013) called for a new view of research, one that is generative and bridges the knowing-doing gap. To Ball, research needs to be aimed at the public good instead of offering large-scale solutions that fail to address real world problems. Others like Donovan (2013) have brought up the idea of using research for school improvement and noted three ways this can be accomplished: 1) change incentives in higher education by encouraging research that focuses less on the theoretical and more on problems of practice (PoPs); 2) develop interdisciplinary teams comprised of researchers, practitioners, and education designers; and 3) use real contexts for study by performing meaningful experimentation in schools. A little later, Gutierrez and Penuel (2014) noted the need for new, innovative approaches for research and development in education, citing the improvement work of Bryk, Gomez, and Grunow (2011) as a prime example. As President of the Carnegie Foundation for the Advancement of Teaching, Bryk (2018) continues to promote this work by advocating for new ways to bridge the growing chasm between research and practice as a necessity to make things better for our most disadvantaged students and communities. Bryk (2018) also advocates for a research and development infrastructure that focuses on improving the learning of all students and doing so quickly through the rapid, iterative testing of change ideas.

To make educational research accessible and useful in practice, the field needs translational researchers, a term used in health care and other professions to describe individuals capable of bridging the research-community divide. Translational health-care workers share information between physicians, nurses, and patients. They move information from the research workbench to the patient's bedside (Bulterman-Bos, 2008; Smith & Helfenbein, 2008). However, to accomplish this kind of fluidity between research and practice, professionals need training that includes:

- transdisciplinary work focused on common problems and opportunities to solve them in multi-disciplinary teams;
- opportunities to use what they know and be original, creative, and innovative;
- common curricula to gain a solid understanding of both research and patient care;
- individualized curricula to expand interests;
- learner-centered faculty and advisory committees; and
- field work that enhances practical knowledge and communication skills (Bulterman-Bos, 2008).

This type of training develops translational researchers who work collaboratively to find practical solutions to everyday problems, make their findings accessible to those who need them, and influence practice, research, and policy. Translational researchers move information from the research workbench to the patient's bedside or cross the theory-to-practice divide (Ball, 2013; Latham, 2008). In education, professional practitioners create coherence between theory, research, and the everyday work in educational organizations.

We believe education needs translational researchers. We see scholarly practitioners who are prepared in EdD programs as these individuals. We also see improvement science as a necessary part of scholarly practitioner training and dissertation work. Though work towards this goal has begun, it is not yet a reality everywhere. Gaps continue to exist between the geography of professional practice and the culture of universities. The flow of work in universities often bears scant resemblance to the rhythms and needs of PK-12 school life (Murphy, 2014b).

What Is Improvement Science?

> Education research would benefit from Improvement Science, which has methods tailored to rapid prototyping and testing, tools for detecting and learning from variation, and affordances to learn from widely different contexts. (Lewis, 2015, p. 59)

Improvement science is a methodological approach built on pragmatism and science that uses disciplined inquiry to solve PoPs. Improvement science focuses on high-leverage problems and the systems that surround those problems. It uses experiential and scholarly knowledge and data to understand if change efforts lead to an improvement (Bryk, Gomez, & Grunow, 2011). This methodology starts small and moves through multiple cycles towards a well-thought-out aim of improvement. The work of improvement science invites everyone affected by the existing problem to collectively learn their way together into stronger performance and better outcomes (Bennett, Grunow, & Meyer, 2018). In these ways, improvement science seemingly fits the needs of educators because it is both practical and rigorous and serves the purpose of a DiP. In EdD programs, improvement science encourages collaboration between students (practitioners) and their faculty, committee members (researchers), and stakeholders (organizational members).

To perform this type of work, the Carnegie Foundation poses Six Core Principles of Improvement (outlined in Chapter 1). Using these principles, the Carnegie Foundation is working with schools and organizations to produce quality outcomes (Bryk, 2018; Bryk, et al., 2011; Bryk, Gomez, Grunow, & LeMahieu, 2015a; LeMahieu, Bryk, Grunow, & Gomez, 2017). CPED has built on this movement to bring improvement science into EdD programs in order to prepare leaders with the skills and abilities of improvement science to address the problems they face.

Practically, improvement science is what educators and organizational leaders do inherently every day: strive to improve their contexts systematically. Often, rather than or alongside implementing top-down mandates or outside reforms, educational practitioners regularly perform actions similar to improvement science, focusing on their own organizational problems (e.g., learning, behavior, motivation, resources), developing their own theories about these problems, and collecting data that inform their own efforts to improve these problems. Improvement science seeks to take this intuitive work a step further and support leaders in answering everyday questions using a systematic, systems-changing discipline inquiry process (Bryk, et al., 2015; Gutierrez & Penuel, 2014). Note Table 2.1 for an explanation of these ideas.

These questions are combined with Plan-Do-Study-Act (PDSA) *90-day* cycles (our version of this will be discussed in Chapter 7) so improvers work iteratively. They plan change efforts, do them,

Table 2.1. Questions Answered by Improvement Science and Reasons for the Questions

Question	Reason for the Question
What is hoped to be accomplish?	To specify, clarify, and contextualize a specific problem.
What changes would result in an improvement? What is the rationale for these?	To generate actionable changes based on the best reasoning and information available.
Why are changes thought to lead to improvement?	To provide a rationale as to why the chosen change ideas makes sense.
How might one recognize if a change led to an improvement?	To develop a process by which data are examined and from this, draw valid and reasoned conclusions about improvements made or not.

study what occurred, and decide on next steps. Working this way lets educators test their own theories within their own contexts and understand what worked, for who, under what circumstances, and why (Bryk, 2018). Improvement science moves research out of laboratory settings and randomized field trials into real world classrooms. Contextualizing improvement work in a dissertation process can create translational researchers who have skills, knowledge, and habits to break the cycle of failed educational reforms (Lewis, 2015; Mehta, et al., 2011).

Despite improvement science being a practical approach that encourages the integration of experiential knowledge with extant theory and applied social science inquiry, it is still a rigorous and scientific methodology. Improvement science is rooted in the work of Deming (1993), who spent much of his career advising corporations on how to create and manage their outcomes, even as they evolved. His idea of *Profound Knowledge* helped organizations realize that four interrelated ideas could help them improve: 1) appreciation of a system, 2) knowledge of variation, 3) theory of knowledge, and 4) psychology. Improvement science, Total Quality Management, Six Sigma, Design-Based Research, and other improvement models rest on Deming's ideas and are being used by professionals in various fields (e.g., healthcare, agriculture, service sectors, manufacturing) to make systems function better (LeMahieu, et al., 2017; Lucas & Nacer, 2015). For the field of education, though improvement science is a fairly new methodology, it is a natural fit to be user centered and focused on high-leverage problems that have multiple interacting causes requiring diverse thinking. Improvement science is also a natural fit for practitioners who are often analogical scavengers, gathering and distributing ideas in thoughtful and precise ways (Carnegie Foundation for the Advancement of Teaching, 2015).

Lucas & Nacer's (2015) habits of health-care improvers (described in Chapter 1) align with the aspirations of professionals in EdD programs as well as the needs of the education profession. Instead of becoming subject area experts or developers of theory, EdD students want to become scholarly practitioners, capable of naming, framing, and solving the complex PoPs they face every day.

Students in EdD programs want to apply what they are learning to move their organizations ahead (Mintrop, 2016). Improvement science meets these goals because it allows students to investigate their own contexts and blend the practical, experiential knowledge they have with the scholarly knowledge they learn in their doctoral programs. EdD students take what they learn from their programs and apply it to their workplace, effectively becoming translational researchers who cross the theory to practice divide. Yet, despite the potential impact these practitioners can have in practice, some faculty, committee members, and others question the legitimacy of improvement science. They demand traditional methods and frames for student dissertations. To counter this hegemonic thinking in support of the needs of practitioners, the naysayers must be convinced that improvement science is scientific.

Is Improvement Science Scientific?

Science is a systematic and logical approach to discovering how things work. It tests theories and ideas and analyzes data based on fact, not opinion or preferences (Bradford, 2017). A science:

- produces a body of knowledge with a process of discovery (the scientific method) that allows the linking of isolated facts into coherent and comprehensive understandings;
- is exciting and motivating. Science encourages critical thinking, innovation, and problems solving;
- is useful, powerful, and reliable. Science develops new procedures, products, and processes;
- is ongoing. Science is never "finished." It continually refines and expands with new questions and ideas; and
- is a global human endeavor. People from every nation engage in science and make contributions to it (The University of California Museum of Paleontology, Berkeley, and the Regents of the University of California, 2013).

Science has these properties and rests on the scientific method, an empirical way of acquiring knowledge. The steps in the method include:

Step 1: asking a question;
Step 2: conducting background research;
Step 3: constructing a hypothesis. Why are things like this?;
Step 4: testing the hypothesis with an experiment; and
Step 5: analyzing the data gathered and draw reasoned conclusions.

Perla, Provost, and Parry (2013) have embraced the idea of improvement science being scientific and we agree with their propositions for several reasons. First, they believe PDSA cycles align with the scientific method because these cycles require a question, several predictions (hypothesis), gathering data to test the prediction, and an unbiased, reasoned way to analyze the data to determine whether the hypothesis was correct or not. In this process, personal theories are balanced with logic and justification. This is thinking scientifically using the scientific process. Second, Perla, Provost, and Parry note that improvement science is nested in the tradition of pragmatism, a frame that focuses on the practical aspects of what works and why. Pragmatics believe: (a) problems and questions are more important than underlying philosophical assumptions; (b) scientific inquiry is contextual in nature—past and current social, historical, and political conditions influence the scientific process; (c) the most effective forms of inquiry are multidisciplinary and multivoiced; and (d) not all findings need to generalize. The third reason Perla, Provost, and Parry believe improvement science is scientific is because of its use of what is known about human behavior and motivation. For example, psychology is used to understand how people learn, why they are motivated, and how they react to change. Systems theory is used to understand the dynamic, adaptiveness of systems and the individuals in them. Finally, improvement science is scientific because it has a common nomenclature (language) that creates a shared understanding. Terms and processes are conceptualized, operationalized, and defined.

Perla, Provost, and Parry (2013) show that improvement science is truly a science and, in our minds, worthy as a dissertation frame. Improvement science focuses on high-leverage problems that necessitate complex thinking. PDSA cycles align with the scientific method and their iterative cycles help educators build new knowledge, products, and processes. Improvement science is nested in traditions that respect local understanding, and it utilizes what is known about human thinking in complex systems. All of these ideas have led us to believe that improvement science would be a good framework for a practitioner's dissertation, or DiP. Still, we acknowledge that accepting improvement science as a scientific process can be challenging in doctoral programs. PhD dissertations remain the gold standard because they are fixed by centuries of tradition (Schuster & Finkelstein, 2006). CPED members are working to change this with innovative ideas about what dissertations mean and should look like (Archbald, 2008, 2010; Kennedy, Altman, & Pizano, 2018; Murphy, 2014a).

PhDs, EdDs, and Dissertations

> The ground of programs and degrees for educational practitioners, whatever the names or titles must be practice. (Murphy, 2014a, p. 24)

The blog Dissertation Hell (http://disshell.blogspot.com) is an online space where doctoral candidates can rant publicly and anonymously about the tortures they have encountered while writing a dissertation. The author created the blog to acknowledge her years of suffering. She, like so many, had reached ABD (All But Dissertation) status and in four years of trying to complete her dissertation only managed to write one chapter. She described the experience as being "incredibly distasteful" (PORKORAMA, 2004).

While not all experiences are bad and not all students blog about it, the fact that platforms like this exist is telling. Dissertations are the most rigorous process doctoral students face in their program as well as the place where many of them fall down. In fact, the attrition rate in PhD programs in the United States has hovered around 50 percent (Cassuro, 2013; Council of Graduate Schools, 2009; Murphy, 2014b). It is a sad fact that many doctoral students complete their coursework but never finish their dissertations and remain ABDs. What is sadder is the lack of change across doctoral education to try and address this.

Why we need distinct dissertations

Attrition rates are dismal in higher education and because the dissertation is where many students fall down, it is worth wondering why. PhD dissertations are designed to transform the doctoral candidate into an academic who will research, teach, and serve their institution and their profession. Given this, PhD dissertations must be original (meaning not researched before), aimed at building or extending theory, and, in most cases, aligned with the major professor's expertise and research. PhD dissertations help students gain mastery of methodological, historical, topical, empirical, and theoretical concepts and in turn, become experts in a defined domain. Dissertation work prepares the PhD candidate to make a significant contribution to the scholarship in their field, earn tenure, and move up the ranks from assistant to associate to full professor (Murphy, 2014b; Nyquist, Woodford, & Rogers, 2004).

In contrast, EdD students are working professionals who want to get a degree and remain in the field. Given this, they want their degree and dissertation work to matter to their personal and professional goals and to the populations they serve (Perry, 2012a, 2012b, 2014, 2016; Shulman et al., 2006). EdD students want to gain the knowledge, skills, and dispositions they need to successfully raise up disadvantaged populations in educational organizations (Bryk, Gomez, Grunow, & LeMahieu, 2015b; Gomez, Russell, Bryk, LeMahieu, & Mejia, 2016). They want to understand the systems and processes that created inequities, learn how to use the mounds of data they receive to help their students learn better, and understand how to build consensus in politically charged times.

However, needs like these are not necessarily addressed through dissertation work. It has been difficult for higher education to let go of the status quo and consider new methods and dissertation frames. Two of the most difficult components to conceptualize and change in EdD programs are the culminating project and associated elements of research preparation (Perry & Abruzzo, in press). Long-standing traditions surrounding the teaching of research and the dissertation's appropriateness, form, content, and completion often preclude any discussion of innovation or alteration (Bengtson & Jones, 2014; Hochbein & Perry, 2013). However, thanks to innovators and advocates some programs are working toward making changes that support professional preparation.

New ideas for programs

Hochbein and Perry (2013) argue for distinct research training in EdD programs because practitioners do not go to graduate school to create new theories or find generalizable solutions but rather want to work in local contexts, change inequities, and use what they learn to solve PoPs. Hochbein and Perry (2013) note that these aspirations require different training and different dissertations. In their words, "Conceptualizing and addressing problems of practice requires a much different skillset than in a traditional dissertation" (Hochbein & Perry, 2013, p. 22). Scholarly practitioners need to learn to decipher existing knowledge and the validity of that knowledge, debate the need for reforms using existing research, and apply the findings of research literature in the design of practical and testable solutions to address pressing PoPs. These skills are vastly different than the skills PhD students need to become researchers or academics.

Such arguments back the notion that EdD programs need to be distinct from PhD programs, which requires new thinking and much change in schools of education. CPED has brought together members of schools of education since 2007 to work to distinguish the EdD as the professional degree in education. In 2014, in an effort to understand if CPED had been impactful, members conducted a cross-case study of 21 of its original member institutions and found that all were working to distinguish their EdDs from their PhDs, to increase enrollment and graduation rates for practitioners, to change their degree structures including time to degree, and to make changes to their dissertations and their advising models. These EdD programs changed in terms of purpose and goals, the types of research preparation, and their reliance on cohort models as means of improving preparation and graduation. A few institutions in the study had started using group dissertations as a distinguishing factor that supported practitioner learning (Crowe, 2013; Perry, 2016; Perry & Imig, 2016; Perry, Zambo, & Wunder, 2015). A while later (2017–2018), more data were gathered from CPED Member Reports (n=53 institutions). These data showed that preparation for completing the culminating product, or the DiP, was woven throughout programs and coursework. Students began working on their dissertations early (often in the first course) and components of the product were added and refined as students traversed toward graduation. Additionally, 83% of respondents noted that self-selected PoPs were the central focus of DiPs and that these problems often focused on social justice, learning, behavior and motivation of students, and teacher development (Abruzzo, Carlins, Zambo, & Bowden, 2019).

Thoughts on EdD dissertations

Scholars have examined the utility of the dissertation for practitioners. For example Joseph Murphy says dissertations are "work that need not be done by those who should not be doing it" (2014a, p. 27). Murphy believes that dissertations corrupt leadership training because to do them, programs focus too much on academics (theory) instead of practice and problems. To Murphy, colleges of education overlook Dewey's essential theme of using educational practice to shape inquiry and action, instead of the other way around. Murphy expounds that education needs to situate scientific evidence in the ways data exist in schools. He suggests dissertations should be portfolio-like and focused on PoPs from clients, situated in everyday work, and performed collaboratively instead of individually. He notes that EdD dissertations should be distinct from PhD dissertations in these three ways.

1. The PhD dissertation should be about specialization and becoming an expert in a defined domain of learning. In contrast, EdD students are generalists. Therefore, course- and dissertation-work should prepare them for this work.
2. The PhD dissertation honors writing for a career of publication, yet EdD students rarely write long narratives (80% of their work is interpersonal). The writing of school leaders bears little resemblance to the academic writing in a dissertation.
3. The PhD dissertation features the consumption of research articles and the conducting of an "original" piece of research, yet EdD students will rarely, if ever, read a research article (as defined by us) and will almost never conduct another research study in their careers (Murphy, 2014b).

Another scholar who has articulated the need to distinguish the EdD dissertations is Douglas Archbald (2014), who posed that problem-solving for organizational improvement should be the goal of culminating projects/capstones and that resulting products should be portfolio-like instead of book-like chapters. To Archbald (2014), capstones should have four qualities: (a) developmental efficacy, (b) community benefit, (c) stewardship of doctoral values, and (d) distinctiveness. He further explains that the writing of dissertations should demonstrate that EdD program graduates have the capability to make better decisions, change practice, and produce better results (Archbald, 2010).

The education field has strong advocates for changing the way research and dissertations are taught for practitioners. Change is happening across many schools of education and conversations about distinctions continue. Still, more work needs to be done as mindset and tradition are slow to change in academia.

Distinguishing the EdD Dissertation

> When the story of preparation is unpacked, it is the EdD students who are consistently damaged. (Murphy, 2014b, p. 25)

The quote above reminds us of the sordid past and confusion surrounding the EdD and its dissertations. Over the past 15 years, there has been a growing concern that the traditional 305+ page dissertation, completed at the end of coursework, does not serve the needs of doctoral students planning professional careers (Shulman et al., 2006; Willis, Inman, & Valenti, 2010). Historically, dissertations in EdD programs have often mirrored PhD dissertations. More recently, faculty from programs associated with CPED have been working collaboratively to define and transform their dissertations into *DiPs*, scholarly endeavors that impact a complex PoP (CPED, 2010). DiPs are different from traditional dissertations in that they focus on addressing PoPs through applied inquiry. They engage inquiry questions rather than research questions to define the role of research in practice. Inquiry questions are those that arise out of practice, are co-constructed, user-centered, focus on diversity, equity, and social justice, and are meaningful to the student and their professional context. Instead of an exhaustive literature review, DiPs have EdD students perform a shorter, targeted Reviews of Scholarly and Professional Knowledge to help name and frame problems using experiential and professional sources. This kind of review helps scholarly practitioners better understand the root and history of their problem, clarify their inquiry questions, find potential solutions, and uncover the best measures to use to understand the impact of their work. DiPs also focus on designing and implementing changes that improve or solve PoPs. That is, a change idea is implemented, data is collected on the results of the implementation, and decisions are made about how to move forward for continuous improvement. Results of the DiP work go beyond the dissertation committee and are often shared with those who can incorporate it into professional practice. Table 2 captures how *DiPs* should differ from PhD dissertations.

Table 2.2. How EdD DiPs Should Differ from PhD Dissertations

	PhD Dissertation	**EdD DIP**
Purpose	extend theory, discover something new	impact a complex problem of practice and self as leader
Questions	research questions—theoretical/academic within one's field or questions other researchers have not considered	Significant, high-leverage questions focused on complex problems of practice that are often framed around equity, ethics, and social justice—problems are user centered and compelling
Literature	comprehensive literature review—in depth review of the historical, contextual, or social foundation of the study	Review of Scholarly and Professional Knowledge—concise review blending professional, practical knowledge with scholarly knowledge to understand the problem, find solutions, and develop measures that will provide evidence of change (or not); scholarly knowledge is deciphered, debated, and used for solutions
Methods	quantitative, qualitative or mixed researcher is an outsider	practical measures and processes aimed at uncovering if the change is working (may be quantitative, qualitative, or mixed)
Analysis	by the researcher with some member checks	by the scholarly practitioner
Spread	published in peer-reviewed journals and presented at conferences	disseminated in various ways—communicated to stakeholders, published in professional and scholarly journals, and presented at conferences
Career	basis of an academic career—start of a publication record	advance professional knowledge and self as a leader

Improvement Science and the DiP

The idea of bringing improvement science into higher education started around 2012 when Anthony Bryk, President of the Carnegie Foundation for Advancement of Teaching, spoke to a group of CPED faculty members about how improvement science and Networked

Improvement Communities (NICs) could be new pathways for conducting research and development in education. At that time, Bryk posed the following questions:

1. What if cadres of EdD candidates across multiple institutions were working on a problem, or parts of a problem, in NICs?
2. What if CPED institutions served as supporting NICs, while also developing human and social capacity for this work to grow?

These questions led to much debate and some pioneer faculty beginning to investigate and teach improvement science in their EdD courses.

A while later, Ash Vasudeva (2017), Vice President of Strategic Initiatives at the Carnegie Foundation for Advancement of Teaching, continued the conversation with CPED faculty by asking them if their existing strategies, approaches and structures were sufficient for the next decade. In his words, "Is what *got* you here today enough to *get* you where you want to go tomorrow?" (Vasudeva, 2017, p. 2) To answer that question, Vasudeva brought up two ideas:

1. the tendency of schools of education to emulate traditional forms of academic research and scholarship; and
2. the tendency to less-than-adequately address the pressing needs of practitioners in schools and school systems, particularly those related to equitable opportunities and outcomes (Judge, 1982).

Both Bryk (2015) and Vasudeva (2017) have prompted further thinking about the role of inquiry in higher education and the change that is needed if practitioners are to be supported.

Building on the ideas from the Carnegie Foundation's promulgation of improvement science as a strategy to better address PoPs and CPED's definition of the DiP, we propose that improvement science be the signature methodology of the DiPs. The ISDiP, as we call it, moves beyond the DiP to offer a systematic methodology and skillset for practitioners to use not only in their EdD program but also (and more importantly) in their professional practice. The ISDiP teaches students to become scholarly practitioners by offering them the skills to:

1. identify an actionable PoP in a local education setting in which the student currently serves;
2. develop a change that is based on the student's professional knowledge along with the best scholarship available;
3. implement and study the change effort systematically and methodically through a disciplined 90-day cycle; and
4. Report findings to both local stakeholders, the doctoral committee, and when appropriate, beyond to other professionals.

In general, the purpose of the ISDiP is to report the consequences of a particular educational improvement effort. The ISDiP is *not* undertaken to develop theory or fill gaps in the knowledge base of a discipline. The image below provides a visual of our idea of an ISDiP.

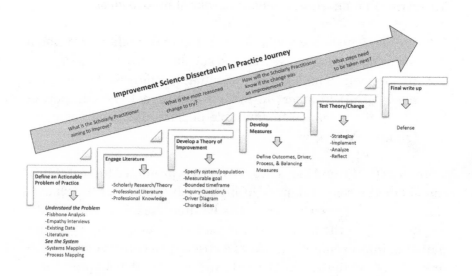

Figure 2.1. ISDiP Journey

In the remainder of this chapter, we provide a brief description of each part of the ISDiP, which form the basis for the rest of the chapters in this book.

Define an actionable PoP

As many of us know, it is important to take time to identify and understand the causes of complex problems before taking any steps. For EdD students, we call such problems actionable PoPs (Mintrop, 2016). The identification process means naming and framing a PoP, or a persistent, contextualized, and specific issue embedded in the work of a professional practitioner, the addressing of which has the potential to result in improved understanding, experience, and outcomes (CPED, 2010). To be actionable means that the problem is within the student's sphere of influence (Mintrop, 2016). Another way to think about an actionable PoP would be to consider the Carnegie Foundation's definition of a high-leverage problem, which is one that 1) consumes substantial resources, 2) has potential for variable outcomes, and 3) if addressed would result in better efficiency and/or effectiveness (Bryk, et al., 2015). However, identifying this type of problem can be challenging (Mintrop, 2016). Students often bring solutions rather than specific problems, but tools like fishbones and systems maps can help to shift the focus back to the problem (Bryk, et al., 2015). Chapter 3 will explain how to find actionable problems using tools like these.

Engage literature

EdD students have a wealth of practical knowledge and because of this, they need to engage with literature differently than PhD students. Instead of writing an exhaustive review of literature that covers the history of their problem, scholarly practitioners write reviews that are targeted, selective, practical, and relevant to their improvement effort. Literature is blended with their practical knowledge and used to improve their leadership capabilities. They decipher the literature, debate its applicability for their own contexts, and apply findings in the design of practical and testable solutions to address pressing PoPs (Hochbein & Perry, 2013). Scholarly practitioners writing ISDiPs use literature to:

- link their problem to universal problems that have been empirically studied;
- justify why their problem matters to practice and to them;
- document what is known (and not known) about the problem in other contexts;
- identify theories that inform the change effort;
- gain models for measures, analysis, and interpreting results; and
- enrich their professional and practical knowledge.

Chapter 4 provides more insight into the use of literature in an ISDiP.

Develop a Theory of Improvement

A Driver Diagram is an improvement tool that visually represents the student's working theory of improvement and creates a common language and vision to coordinate efforts among individuals (Bryk, 2018; Bryk, et al., 2015; Milder & Lorr, 2019). It is based on the student's goals for improving their PoP, the identification of leverage points in their system where change might be possible, and the posing of potential solutions to improve not only the problem but the organizational system. Driver Diagrams contain an aim, primary drivers (hypothesis on what to target), secondary drivers (sub-hypothesis), and change ideas. The use of Driver Diagrams in developing a working theory of improvement will be further explained in Chapter 5.

Develop measures

> We cannot improve at scale what we cannot measure. (Bryk, et al., 2015, p. 87)

The next step in the ISDiP process is to develop and explain the measures that will be used to determine if a change was an improvement. The quote above from Byrk, et al., (2015) suggests that this step has many components. Improvers know that measures are the "north star" in any effort and that you cannot improve something if you cannot measure the visible change (Bryk, et al., 2015). Explaining measures needs to be explicit. Each measure must be clearly described including why the particular measure will be used, how it will be used, and how it will be analyzed. Measures for improvement should be transparent, rigorous, and fit into the everyday workings of the context where the PoP is situated. Measures for improvement are used to answer four questions:

1. Is the change working? (driver measures)
2. How is it working? (process measures)
3. Is it working as intended? (balancing measures)
4. Did it work? (outcome measures) (Hinnant-Crawford, 2019)

These questions illustrate how measurement for improvement does not provide data to develop grand theories or generalizable results. Measurement for improvement is culled from the work of practice and fits into it instead of the other way around (Murphy, 2014b). Chapter 6 will provide more insight into these ideas.

Test the theory/change

Testing the change idea is often the most exciting part of the ISDiP for students because this is the time when they get to apply all that they have learned to change their PoP. Testing is undertaken utilizing a 90-day cycle, which, for the ISDiP, we envision as strategizing (S), implementing (I), analyzing (A), and reflecting (R). Implementing a 90-day cycle requires flexibility and strong leadership skills to ensure success. Chapter 7 will explain more.

Summary

Building on ideas from Chapter 1, this chapter has extended the notion of developing scholarly practitioners who work as translational researchers, individuals who, through inquiry into their practice, bridge the theory to practice divide. This chapter also explained that improvement science is a science that uses the scientific method and relies on psychology, systems theory, and pragmatism. We have married improvement science with the DiP to present a visual framework for how improvement work is designed and performed as part of an EdD program. Performing improvement science for dissertation work develops in the practitioner the knowledge, skills, and habits necessary to lead the changes our schools and organizations need. The experience also produces practitioner-generated professional knowledge.

Post-reading questions for faculty

1. Think about your dissertations. How is the work performed? What do your students learn by doing this work? What happens to the work once the dissertation is defended?
2. How would your answers to the above questions differ if your students did an ISDiP?

Post-reading questions for scholarly practitioners/students

1. How is improvement science scientific and how could it be used as a dissertation frame?
2. This chapter provided insight into translational researchers. Describe how this idea aligns with your professional goals. Why would an ISDiP make you better at bridging the theory to practice divide?

References

Abruzzo, E., Carlins, C., Zambo, D., & Bowden, R. (June 2019). Understanding elements of a CPED-influenced dissertation. Handout presented at CPED's June Convening, Lincoln NE.

Archbald, D. (2008). Research versus problem solving for the education leadership doctoral thesis: Implications for form and function. *Educational Administration Quarterly, 44*,(5), 704–739.

Archbald, D. (2010). "Breaking the mold" in the dissertation: Implementing a problem-based, decision-oriented thesis project. *The Journal of Continuing Higher Education, 58*(2), 99–107. https://doi.org/10.1080/07377361003617368

Archbald, D. (2014). *Evolution of a problem-based, improvement-focused EdD capstone: Theory and practice.* Presentation at CPED's June Convening, Denver, CO.

Ball, A. (2013). To know is not enough: Knowledge, power, and the zone of generativity. *Educational Researcher, 41*(8), 283–293. https://doi.org/10.3102/0013189X12465334

Bengtson, E. & Jones, S.J. (2014). *FIPSE product: Research courses in the CPED phase I institutions: What's the difference?* Carnegie Project on the Education Doctorate: Author.

Bennett, B., Gunrow, A., & Meyer, A. (2018). *Improvement Science 101.* Presentation at the Carnegie Foundation for the Advancement of Teaching's Annual Summit, San Francisco, CA.

Berwick, D.M. (2008). The science of improvement. *The Journal of the American Medical Association, 299*(10), 1182–1184.

Bowen, W.G., & Rudenstine, N.L. (1992). *In pursuit of the PhD.* Princeton University Press: Princeton, NJ.

Bradford, A. (2017). What is Science? *Live Science.* Retrieved 8 November 2019, from: https://www.livescience.com/20896-science-scientific-method.html

Bryk, A.S. (2018, April 3). *Advancing quality in continuous improvement.* Speech presented at the Carnegie Foundation Summit on Improvement in Education, San Francisco, CA.

Bryk, A.S, Gomez, L.M., & Grunow, A., (2011). Getting ideas into action: Building networked improvement communities in education. Retrieved

12 December 2019, from http://www.carnegiefoundation.org/spotlight/webinar-bryk-gomez-building-networked-improvement-communities-in-education

Bryk, A.S., Gomez, L.M., Gunrow, A., & LeMahieu, P.G. (2015a). Breaking the cycle of failed school reforms: Using network improvement communities to learn fast and implement well. *Harvard Education Letter, 31*(1), 1–3.

Bryk, A.S., Gomez, L.M., Gunrow, A., & LeMahieu, P.G. (2015b). *Learning to improve*. Harvard College, Cambridge, MA.

Bulterman-Bos, J.A. (2008). Will a clinical approach make education research more relevant for practice? *Educational Researcher, 37*(7), 412–420.

Carnegie Foundation for the Advancement of Teaching. (2015). *Our ideas*. Available from: https://www.carnegiefoundation.org/our-ideas/

Carnegie Project on the Education Doctorate. (2010). *CPED Design Concepts*. College Park, MD: Author.

Cassuro, I. (2013). Ph.D. attrition: How much is too much? *The Chronicle of Higher Education*, available at http://chronicle.com/article/Ph.D.-Attrition-How-Much-Is/140045/

Cesari, J.P. (1990). Thesis and dissertation support groups: A unique service for graduate students. *Journal of College Student Development, 31*(3), 375–376.

Clandinin, J., & Connelly, M. (1995). *Teachers' professional knowledge landscapes*. New York, Teachers College Press.

Council of Graduate Schools. (2007). CGS taskforce report on the professional doctorate. Washington, DC: Author.

Council of Graduate Schools (2009). PhD completion and attrition: Findings from exit surveys of PhD completers. Author.

Crowe, E., (2013). Redesigning the professional doctorate in education year 3 evaluation report. Carnegie Project on the Education Doctorate. Author.

Deming, W.E. (1993). *The new economics for industry, government, education*. The MIT Press: Cambridge, MA.

Donovan, M.S. (2013). Generating improvement through research and development in education. *Science, 304*(6130), 317–319.

Gomez, L.M., Russell, J.L., Bryk, A.S., LeMahieu, P.G., & Mejia, E.M. (2016). The right network for the right problem. *Phi Delta Kappan, 98*(3), 8–15.

Gutierrez, K.D., & Penuel, W.R. (2014). Relevance to practice as a criterion for rigor. *Educational Researcher, 43*(1), 19–23.

Hinnant-Crawford, B. (2019). Practical measurement in improvement science. In Crow, Hinnant-Crawford, and Spalding (Eds) *The educational leader's guide to improvement science: Data, design and cases for reflection.* Myers Education Press, Gorham, ME.

Hochbein, C. & Perry, J.A. (2013) The Role of research in the professional doctorate. *Planning and Changing Journal. 44*(3/4), 181–194.

Judge H. (1982). American graduate schools of education: A view from abroad. New York, NY: Ford Foundation.

Kennedy, B., Altman, M., & Pizano, A. (2018). Engaging in the battle of the snails by challenging the traditional dissertation model. *Impacting Education, 3*(1). https://doi.org/10.5195/ie.2018.27

Langley, G., Moen, R., Nolan, K., Nolan, T., Norman, C., & Provost, L. (2009). *The improvement guide: A practical approach to enhancing organizational performance* (2nd ed.). San Francisco, CA: Jossey-Bass.

Latham, J.R. (2008). Building bridges between researchers and practitioners: A collaborative approach to research in performance excellence. *Quality Management Journal, 15*(1), 20.

LeMahieu. P.G., Bryk, A.S., Grunow. A., Gomez, L.M. (2017). Working to improve: seven approaches to improvement science in education. *Quality Assurance in Education, 25*(1), 2–4.

Lewis, C. (2015) What is improvement science? Do we need it in education? *Educational Researcher, 44*(1), 54–61.

Lucas, B. & Nacer, H. (2015). *The habits of an improver: Thinking about learning for improvement in health care.* The Health Foundation.

Mehta, J., Gomez, L.M., &. Bryk, A.S. (2011). Teaching as a knowledge profession. *Education Week, 30*(26), 27–36.

Milder, S., & Lorr, B. (2019). *Improvement science handbook: Empowering NYC educators to make progress on critical issues that stand in the way of student success.* NYC Department of Education.

Mintrop, R. (2016). *Design-based school improvement: A practical guide for education leaders.* Cambridge, MA: Harvard Education Press.

Murphy, J. (2014a). Insights about the profession: Questionable norms and the marginalization of practice. *On the Horizon, 22*(3), 192–198.

Murphy, J. (2014b Winter). Of questionable value: The EdD dissertation: An essay. *UCEA Review, 55*(1), 27–28.

Nyquist, J.D., Woodford, B.J., and Rogers, D.L. (2004). Re-envisioning the Ph.D: A challenge for the twenty-first century. In D.H. Wulff and A.E. Austin (eds.), *Paths to the professoriate: Strategies for enriching the preparation of future faculty* (pp. 194–216). San Francisco: Jossey-Bass.

Perla, R.J., Provost, L.P., Parry, J.G., (2013). Seven propositions of the science of improvement: Exploring foundations. *Quality Management in Health Care, 22*(3), 170–186. https://doi.org/10.1097/QMH.0b013e31829a6a15

Perry, J.A. (2012a). To Ed.D. or not to Ed.D. *Phi Delta Kappan, 94*(1), 41–44.

Perry, J.A. (2012b). *The EdD and scholarly practitioners: The CPED path.* Charlotte, NC, IA.

Perry, J.A. (2014). The CPED claim: A counter-response. *UCEA Review 55*(1), 22–24.

Perry, J.A. (2016). The scholarly practitioner as steward of the practice. In Storey, V. & Hesbol K. (Eds). *Contemporary approaches to dissertation development and research methods.* Hershey, PA: IGI Global.

Perry, J.A. & Abruzzo, E. (in press). *Preparing the scholarly practitioner: The importance of socialization in CPED-influenced EdD programs.* In Weidman, J.C. & DeAngelo, L. (in press). Socialization in higher education and the early career: Theory, research and application. New York: Springer.

Perry, J.A. & Imig, D. (2016). What do we mean by impact? *Impacting Education. 1*(1), 1–3. https://doi.org/10.5195/ie.2016.26

Perry, J.A., Zambo, D., & Wunder, S. (2015). Understanding how schools of education have redesigned the doctorate of education. *Journal of School Public Relations, 36*(1), 58–85.

PORKORAMA, (2004, December 28). Dissertation hell: Too many years of hell. http://disshell.blogspot.com/2004/12/too-many-years-of-hell.html

Resnick, L. (1999). Making America smarter. *Education Week Century Series, 18*(40), 38–40.

Schuster, J., & Finkelstein, M. (2006). *The American faculty: The restructuring of academic work and careers.* Baltimore, MD: Johns Hopkins Press.

Shulman, L.S. (2005). Signature pedagogies in the professions. *Daedalus, 134*(3), 52–59.

Shulman, L.S., Golde, C.M., Bueschel, A.C., & Garabedian, K.J. (2006). Reclaiming education's doctorates: A critique and a proposal. *Educational Researcher, 35*(3), 25–32.

Smith, J.S., & Helfenbein, R.J. (2008). Translational research in education. In W.S. Gershon (Ed.), *The collaborative turn: Working together in qualitative research*, p. 89–102 Sense Publishers, Rotterham, The Netherlands.

The University of California Museum of Paleontology, Berkeley, and the Regents of the University of California. (2013). *What is science? Understanding Science*. Retrieved 2 December 2019 from www.understandingscience.org

Vasudeva, A. (2017) Reflections and new directions on CPED's 10th anniversary. *Impacting education, 2*(1), 1–5.

Willis, J., & Inman, D., & Valenti, R. (2010). *Completing a professional practice dissertation: A guide for students and faculty*. Information Age Publishing, NC.

Yeager, D., Bryk, A., Muhich, J., Hausman, H., Morales, L. (2014). *Practical measurement*. Carnegie Foundation for the Advancement of Teaching. Retrieved 27 October 2019 from http://cdn.carnegiefoundation.org/wp-content/uploads/2014/09/Practical_Measurement_Yeager-Brykl.pdf

CHAPTER THREE

Actionable Problems of Practice

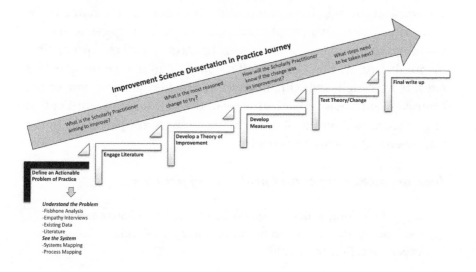

Figure 3.1. Improvement Science Dissertation in Practice (ISDiP) Journey Defining Actionable Problems of Practice

Problem solving lies at the heart of scholarly practitioner work. Practitioners attempt to solve tough educational problems. However, going about the process of problem solving in a systematic fashion requires tools, such as the tools of improvement science. Improvement tools assist the scholarly practitioner in problem identification so that "solutionitis," the propensity to jump to a solution before the problem is known, is avoided (Bryk, et al., 2015). This chapter adds to the foundational knowledge of improvement science as a methodology provided in earlier chapters for understanding why and how the ISDiP can address the types of problems of practice society needs solved.

In this chapter, faculty, mentors, and students will gain insight into how improvement research focused on actionable problems of practice is in sharp contrast to the type of problem focus found in traditional PhD-style dissertations. As a capstone product in doctoral leadership programs, the ISDiP illustrates the component processes of naming and framing an educational issue or dilemma determined to be a universal problem of practice. Because part of the work of the scholarly practitioner is to define actionable problems of practice, this chapter explains the initial stages of understanding the problem and seeing the system parts responsible for producing it. The chapter offers specific guidance on how this work is accomplished. Our discussion provides an overview of the improvement tools specifically related to problem identification and exploration, and explains why these tools are pertinent to the improvement research process.

Improvement science and problems of practice

> A good question is like a beautiful painting. It has boundaries—a focal point that is interpretable and meaningful, related to one's experience. (Mintrop, 2016)

The quote above by Mintrop notes that the heart of the dissertation in practice (DiP) is inextricably tied to the educational problem; the object of the DiP masterpiece. In fact, the ISDiP narrative fully describes an improvement project aimed at combatting problems occurring in practice and spells out the connection between problem solving and the human and material resources needed for solving it. In light of the question, *"What does better look like?"* improvement science offers the practitioner a framework for being deliberative, scientific, and rigorous in the process of achieving the ultimate goal, solving problems to achieve quality, reliably at scale (Bryk, et al., 2015). The ISDiP methodology uniquely responds to the need to not only address troubling practice problems, but to inform the understanding of that practice as an act of scholarly leadership.

The questions improvement science is designed to answer

Because work done in the ISDiP focuses on problems within a leader's organization, the issue to be addressed is one that is perceived by not only the leader, but to the school or institution, and among relevant stakeholders as "significant, persistent, and worthy of investigation" (Gutiérrez & Penuel, 2014, p. 20). From the 30,000-foot perspective, improvement science considers two very broad questions: *What is the problem?* and *What should be done about it?* Problems are created by the design of systems, and because system output varies, corresponding variance in human and other social phenomenon results (Mintrop, 2016). As such, the question of *What is the problem?* can be answered by using improvement science methods.

The ISDiP is also conducted in response to another set of essential questions, those comprising the Model for Improvement (Langley et al., 2009): 1) What are we trying to accomplish? 2) What change can we make that will result in improvement? and 3) How will we know that a change is an improvement? The model's three guiding questions then move the action into inquiry cycles—a scheme that undergirds all improvement research regardless of topic of initiative. These improvement questions are different from the types of traditional research questions typically used in traditional PhD dissertations. In light of the first guiding question from the Model for Improvement, *What are we trying to accomplish?*, backward mapping from the desired results can yield the articulation of a problem statement. When crafting problem statements, practitioners should consider both the problem scope and specificity, bearing in mind the consequences of formulating too broad a focus, rendering the problem unimprovable.

In contrast to traditional PhD theses that generally focus on theory building or filling gaps in conceptual knowledge, note Table 3.1. Practice-based theses use improvement questions to represent intention, manipulation/change, and evaluation of relative successes toward improving problems. Further, improvement questions are crafted to fit both context and contingency involved in the initiative. To do so, one "develops a perspective on the problem and appropriately leads others to frame the problem in a way that enables the organization to design and implement appropriate interventions" (Lomotey, 2018, p. 6).

Table 3.1. Examples of Traditionally-Focused Research Questions

> A research question is the question around which research is centered. It should be clear—provide enough specifics that one's audience can easily understand its purpose without needing additional explanation.
>
> **Qualitative:**
>
> How or what is the _____ (story, meaning of the phenomena, theory, culture-sharing pattern) explain _____ (central phenomena) for _____ (participants) at _____ (study site)?
>
> **Quantitative:**
>
> What is the frequency and variation of x on _____ (name the variable) for _____ (participants)? Does _____ (theory) explain the relationship between _____ (independent variable) and _____ (dependent variable) controlling for the effects of _____ (control variable)?

Another comparison of improvement science questions with more traditional, empirically-oriented research question follows. Note Table 3.2.

Table 3.2. A Comparison of Types of Research Questions

Quantitative Research	Qualitative Research	Improvement Science
Research questions seek cause/effect answers or association among variables.	Research questions seek exploration, explanation, and experience.	Improvement questions are problem-specific/ user-centered and stem from a working theory of improvement.

Actionable Problems of Practice

Problems of practice (PoPs) are defined as "persistent, contextualized, and specific [to an] issue, embedded in the work of a professional practitioner, the addressing of which has the potential to result in improved understanding, experience, and outcomes" (CPED, 2010). PoPs are ill-structured and complex. Identifying PoPs involves "thoughtful and considered approaches to issues relevant to professional practice" (Willis, et al., 2010, p. 44). Improvement work is typically focused on processes and products that either consume resources, are variable, or, if changed, would improve resource efficiency and effectiveness.

Several important elements define the actionable PoP. A major emphasis when exploring PoPs includes the perceived need by individuals affected by the problem. Improvement science techniques allow for the scholarly practitioner to be proactive, inclusive, and collaborative with relevant stakeholders. Furthermore, the problem must be conceptualized in a way that makes it actually improvable. That is, the problem is large enough to be of strategic concern to the organization, yet limited enough in its nature that concrete and tangible improvements can be feasibly attempted and evaluated. Similarly, improvement science techniques allow for determining appropriate pathways for improvement that consider leverage, value, and capacity to affect change. But how to find the right-sized problem can be tricky. In his work on design-based improvement, Mintrop (2016) began to articulate strategies for considering the problem. We have taken his descriptions and adapted them for the ISDiP. Note Table 3.3.

The actionable problems scholarly practitioners focus on are localized and influenced by many factors, such as ethics, positionality within the organization, and available timeframe. Practitioners must consider the appropriateness of their PoPs within their organization. Frequently, the practitioner is in a position relative to those involved in the improvement initiative. In many cases, collaborators may be in subordinate positions. The inherent hierarchy of the organizational structure may lead to ethical considerations arising during the problem identification and selection phase. Factors such as influence, pressure, and even coercion could become involved, particularly in instances where the power differential is abused. Consideration of problem appropriateness and its relation to context is of extreme importance. Signals and other feedback from stakeholders should be considered when assessing the relative

Table 3.3. An Improvement Science Lens for Actionable PoPs. Adapted from Mintrop, 2016.

Actionable PoPs from an Improvement Science Perspective	
Urgent for the organizational leadership	Problem arises out of a perceived need by organizational leadership and can be sourced out of existing institutional data or linked to specific initiatives such as local, district, and state-level mandates
Actionable	Problem exists within the individual's sphere of influence wherein a collaborative approach leads to democratization during problem situating
Feasible	Problem prioritization can occur where change efforts are addressed in a limited timeframe given the available resources
Strategic	Problem is connected to the goals of individuals affected by the challenge within the larger organization and is couched in strategic initiatives and other institutional and governing priorities
Tied to a specific set of practices	Problem is narrowed to specific practice(s) that have a chance of improvement and is assessed through *plan-do-study-act* (PDSA) cycles wherein incremental efforts at change yield new learning
Forward-looking	Problem reaches towards the next level of work in both scaling up practice and in pathways for sustainability wherein work done is not lost in institutional memory but is embedded in policy, procedure, or other cultural/institutional fabric

significance of the problem in relation to other persistent problems also present within the organization.

Where do scholarly practitioners look to discover educational problems? Where do problems of practice originate? Problem sources derive from a variety of areas. Problems may originate from within the organization, or they may arise from those who are affected by it; the stakeholders themselves. Improvement science tools allow for the systematic process of discovering problems of practice. Several tools can be used during this initial stage of *understanding the problem*.

In the improvement journey, scholarly practitioners rely on roadmaps for determining the pathway to accomplish the goals desired. This type of work "starts with the evidence-based identification of a problem of practice" (Lomotey, 2018, p. 6). Aligned with, and supportive of, leaders as change agents, improvement frameworks equip scholarly practitioners with tools to uncover and identify evidence about systemic problems encountered in everyday practice. Improvement work spotlights the causal agents responsible for problematic outcomes and witnessed inequities. The tools of improvement help uncover pervasive problems so the practitioner does not have to start with a blank slate. For example, a systems map (note Figure 3.2) helps to focus on the existing system in order to reveal processes that may become the initial starting point for improvement work to begin. Instead of focusing on the symptom, the practitioner drills down to deconstruct the problem into contributory components so that root causes for the persistent problem are identified.

See the system producing the problem

System, process, and causal mapping are all improvement techniques that allow the scholarly practitioner to "see the system that is responsible for producing the problem" (Bryk, 2015, p. 57) and to avoid solutionitis. Organizational problems arising from fluxuations in system processes can be identified by employing a system improvement map. Note Figure 3.2. System maps allow the practitioner to achieve a deeper level of understanding about the problem situation by clearly defining the problem context.

In this example, the student and colleagues design a system map to determine the factors influencing high school early graduation. Here, the system improvement map is broken down into the four categories of system processes, information infrastructure, human relations, and governance. Developing and using this map would help the EdD student understand the essential features of the system that potentially contribute to the outcomes we see. The student could identify areas within the map that are underperforming and thus potentially narrow the gap between actual and ideal outcomes (Archbald, 2014). The system improvement map is useful in parsing an organization into levels or categories at which activity occurs.

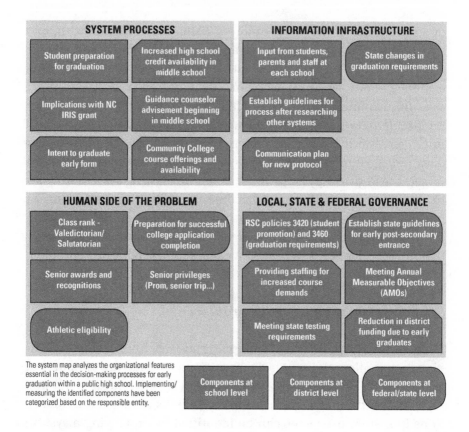

Figure 3.2. System Map for Early High School Graduation

In doing so, the educational leader can then determine which components are priorities, where one might expect to get the most leverage, and what spheres of influence could potentially maximize impact.

Determining the scope of actionable problems

It is essential that an understanding of the parameters of the problem be achieved. Problems of practice are typically obtuse, complex, and multi-dimensional. It is helpful to consider the defining characteristics of the PoP. Problems are user-centered in that they generally pertain to system effects on constituents and stakeholders. PoPs are compelling and have been described as "wicked" in that they are ill-structured and convoluted. Figure 3.3 provides a conceptual lens for thinking about how to narrow the problem into an actionable improvement initiative.

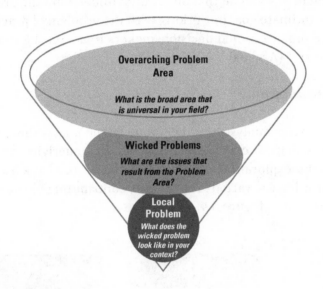

Figure 3.3. Conceptual Framework for Narrowing PoPs

To ensure that practitioner work is focused on problematized situations that are indeed improvable, the level of problem specificity must be articulated: "[The] key to success is getting very clear about the specific problem to be solved" (Bryk et al., 2015, p. 23). To narrow the scope when working with an actionable problem of practice, setting the parameters of the context involves collaboration and input from relevant stakeholders. Too broad of a scope will yield ambiguity and vagueness in purpose. Therefore, careful consideration for crafting an actionable problem must include narrowing to make the problem situation improvable. To effectively negotiate problems in their complexity, it is good practice to deconstruct complex problems into their sub-problem component parts. Opportunities that involve observation of actual processes allow for one to monitor the system, the flow and organization of process elements, and for the detection of anomaly in its output. What practices are happening in the organization currently that signal the problem is occurring? Practitioners need enough investigative space to explore the problem without being so narrow that they miss the problem or so broad that one cannot understand the problem at all: "The ultimate goal in working with the problem of practice is to persuade organizational decision-makers to act on the problem in certain ways" (Archbald, 2008, p. 714).

Fishbone diagrams

Causal systems analysis is a technique which allows those affected by the problem to explore and uncover its underlying causes. To conduct this exploration, a fishbone diagram is used as a framework for illustrating the various root causes contributing to the problem of practice. Note Figure 3.4.

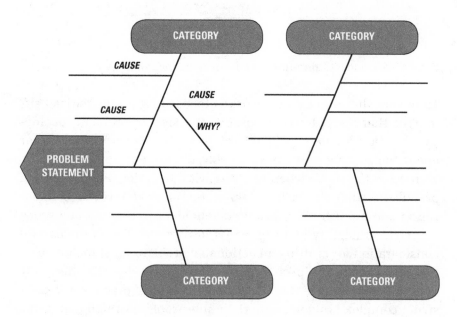

Figure 3.4. Structure of a Causal Systems Diagram

Steps in using the causal analysis first start with identifying the problem. The "head of the fish" in the diagram represents the problem being addressed as a problem statement. Next, the major categories of factors contributing to the problem's existence are represented on the larger "bones of the fish" depicted in the diagram. The number of major categories for a causal map should be between three and eight. Finally, the minor contributing causes within each major category are placed under each category on the smaller bones. The causal systems diagram allows for the visual organization and depiction of possible root causes found to perpetuate a problem of practice. The diagram's structure serves to visually illustrate the underlying factors contributing to the problem's existence.

The process of constructing a fishbone diagram is useful for discovering, organizing, and summarizing the current knowledge surrounding the various causes contributing to the problem's existence. The practice of co-creating the schematic allows collaborators to contribute towards building a shared understanding of the problem's root causes by serving as a mechanism through which multiple perspectives can be elicited and recorded. Working through "why" questions—*Why are we getting the outcomes we currently have?*—as a strategy promotes an understanding of the problem's causes well before solutions are sought. As a rule, one must first determine the root causes of a problem of practice in order to then determine possible strategies for addressing it. Explored in later chapters is a discussion on translating elements from the causal analysis into a driver diagram for action.

Existing organizational data

Other useful strategies exist for identifying problems of practice. A likely source for pointing to organizational problems is in the existing data. Institutional data can illustrate problem areas present within the organizational environment. Data can be particularly useful for illuminating the existence of issues in regard to equity and access. Data mining, analytics, and other analyses of system output may reveal anomalies that exist for certain people, under certain conditions, and in certain contexts. In the form of organizational output, data can also yield information describing the present systemic conditions in relation to the set of conditions that are ultimately desired. Gaining an understanding about the gap between the actual situation and the ideal situation is a good strategy for uncovering problems for improvement work. Practitioners start by defining the initial state of the problem in context, and then seek to determine the desired state. For example, a school district's initiative to combat bullying behaviors might begin by collecting the existing data on the current status of referrals, suspensions, and other discipline-related matters prior to formulating potential interventions. Establishing baseline data, such as in this example, allows one to later determine whether changes implemented "moved the needle" towards the ideal state.

Problems and literature

The published research literature is yet another excellent source of information for informing a problem area. Doctoral students should consult the empirical literature base and utilize research findings from published studies, coupled with their own learning and experiences, to aid in establishing clarity and insight into the contributing factors, or root causes, underlying problems of practice. Literature, blended with professional knowledges, helps the student develop an understanding of the surroundings and innerworkings of the problem situation. Empirical knowledge from the field not only yields tangible information to enable practitioners to avoid solutionitis, but can also "locate the problem in a wider social discourse" (Groundwater-Smith & Mockler, 2007, p. 1).

Observations and empathy interviews

Observational methods focused on day-to-day operations can assist in yielding information that demonstrates variation in processes. In an effort to further understand the ramifications related to the problem, follow-up empathy interviews can be used to reach a deeper appreciation of how culture and context influence the stakeholders' perspective around the problem. Empathy interviews are designed to better understand stakeholders or users by getting insight into their view of the problem, appreciating their perspectives as individuals, understanding how they feel about the problem, and communicating an understanding of their perspective. The Stanford d.school has proposed an empathy interview (Barry, n.d.) to include the following elements:

1. Introducing oneself
2. Introducing the project/problem of practice
3. Building rapport
4. Evoking stories
5. Exploring emotions
6. Asking follow up questions/statements
7. Thanking and wrapping up

Such insights from stakeholders or users can contribute greatly to the scholarly practitioner's understanding of a problem because it moves them beyond their own experience and views.

Together, the two methods of observation and interview can be used in this phase as these techniques allow the practitioner to identify the ways problems affecting stakeholders might need attention. To actualize the improvement principle, *understand the problem*, documentation of analyses of observations can be collected over time. For example, a run chart is helpful in documenting observations of system output prior to implementing an intervention (Perla, et al., 2013). Pre-intervention data collection allows for plotting trends before any improvements are initiated. Knowing *a priori* about a problem and its presenting behaviors preceding improvement work is helpful for determining, and can provide evidence substantiating, whether changes subsequent to your initiative getting underway are indeed improvements.

Process mapping

Once the existence of the problem has been established, information gleaned from engaging in various improvement science frameworks allows for the educational leader to dig deeper into the problem occurring in the system. Because "learning often comes from understanding the themes and patterns in the data" (Langley, et al., 2009, p. 30), a technique found to be particularly relevant to this phase of problem understanding is process mapping. Process mapping allows one to discover bottlenecks and other barriers contributing to the variation that exists in system output due to the design of the system. The strategy for problem detection occurs when one sees anomalies present in process mapping data. In identifying and labeling each component part in the process, even the interactions occurring between the component parts, data can then be collected that pinpoints specific areas affected within the system process.

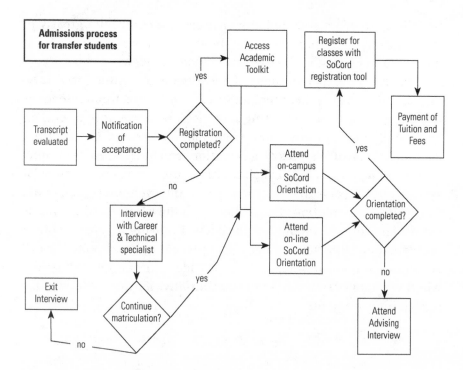

Figure 3.5. Example of Process Map for Transfer Student College Admissions

For example, in order to locate obstacles and other challenges occurring within the process of transferring enrollment, a process map of the community college admissions procedure (note Figure 3.5) allows one to consider the system's components and how these elements influence and contribute to the maladies we see occurring in the process outcome/output measures. Drilling down into process elements is done in an effort to generate data about bottlenecks and other points of process breakdown. In gathering evidence that a problem investigation and subsequent improvement initiative is warranted, perceptions of faculty, students, and staff might be assessed by creating an interactive "hotspot" survey form, wherein elements in the admissions process could be selected with a simple mouse-click. This type of interactive survey could be administered to relevant stakeholders so that those affected could pinpoint specific areas that are presenting challenges. These data can then be aggregated and used as part of the body of evidence for justifying recommendations for improving specific areas within the college admissions process found to be in need of attention.

Summary

The work of improvement focuses in on a *specific problem* to be solved, and the defining characteristics of this problem are anchored in a deep understanding of the experiences of people actually engaged in the work. We call this idea being *user-centered* (Bryk, 2018). Improving educational and organizational problem situations is no easy task. To be successful in this work, the practitioner must have processes, tools, and a flexible approach in mind. Identifying the organizational problem leads one into a problem-solving journey, a scheme characterizing the DiP. Several elements should be considered as one prepares to engage in working with PoPs. First, there should be a solid case built, where argumentation and evidence demonstrate that the work is warranted; that indeed, the problem exists. Archbald (2008) calls this "persuasion, not proof" (p. 714) whereby the definition of a problem is aimed at persuading organizational leaders of the gravity of the problem and the need to take action. Second, in case building, evidence is gathered and collected from various locations, and once organized, becomes the substance comprising the rationale that work on the problem is indeed warranted. Lastly, the scholarly practitioner in the ISDiP builds a case using existing data to demonstrate that a problem is occurring. Together, these skills of making claims about a problem and supporting that claim with evidence not only defines the PoP, but gives the scholarly practitioner the opportunity to internalize, develop, and build a repertoire for a collection of methods for ensuring success as organizational change agents.

Post-reading questions for faculty

1. How might a system map or a fishbone diagram enrich the learning, work, and dissertations of scholarly practitioners?
2. How would these two tools help students understand the systems, roles, processes, and policies surrounding their problems of practice?

Post-reading questions for scholarly practitioners/students

1. Pick an improvement tool and explain how you might use it to "understand the problem."
2. Construct either a process or a system map illustrating the context of your PoP. Which elements do you have the most leverage or control over and which elements do you not? Explain.

References

Archbald, D. (2008). Research versus problem solving for the education leadership doctoral thesis: Implications for form and function. *Educational Administration Quarterly, 44*(5), 704–739.

Archbald, D. (2014). *The GAPPSI Method: Problem-solving, planning, and communicating: Concepts and strategies for leadership in education.* Ypsilanti, MI: National Council of Professors of Educational Administration Press.

Barry, M. (n.d.). *Interview for empathy.* http://dschool-old.stanford.edu/wp-content/themes/dschool/method-cards/interview-for-empathy.pdf

Bryk, A. (2018). Advancing quality in continuous improvement. Keynote speech presented at the Carnegie Foundation Summit on Improvement in Education, San Francisco, CA.

Bryk, A., Gomez, L., Grunow, A., & LeMahieu, P. (2015). *Learning to improve: How America's schools can get better at getting better.* Cambridge, MA: Harvard Education Press.

CPED. (2010). *The CPED Framework.* https://www.cpedinitiative.org/the-framework

Dirkx, J. (2006). Studying the complicated matter of what works: Evidence-based research and the problem of practice. *Adult Education Quarterly, 56*(4), 273–290.

Groundwater-Smith, S., & Mockler, N. (2007). Ethics in practitioner research: An issue of quality. *Research Papers in Education, 22*(2), 199–211. https://doi.org/10.1080/02671520701296171

Gutiérrez, K., & Penuel, W. (2014). Relevance to practice as a criterion for rigor. *Educational Researcher, 43*(1), 19–23.

Langley, G., Moen, R., Nolan, K., Nolan, T., Norman, C., & Provost, L. (2009). *The improvement guide: A practical approach to enhancing organizational performance (2nd ed.).* San Francisco, CA: Jossey-Bass.

LeMahieu, Paul G. and Nordstrum Lee, E. (2016) *Working to improve: Seven approaches to quality improvement in education.* Carnegie Foundation for the Advancement of Teaching. Stanford, CA.

Lomotey, K. (2018). *The disquisition at Western Carolina University: The capstone experience in the University's EdD program.* Unpublished manuscript, Western Carolina University, Cullowhee, NC.

Mintrop, H. (2016). *Design-based school improvement: A practical guide for education leaders.* Cambridge, MA: Harvard Education Press.

Perla, R., Provost, L., Murry, S. (2011). The run chart: A simple analytical tool for learning from variation in healthcare processes. *BMJ Quality & Safety, 20*(1), 46–51.

Willis, J., Inman, D., & Valenti, R. (2010). *Completing a professional practice dissertation: A guide for doctoral students and faculty.* Charlotte, NC: Information Age Publishing.

CHAPTER FOUR

Reviewing the Literature:

A Critical Skill

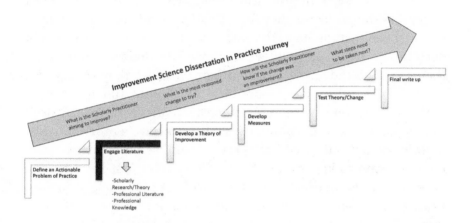

Figure 4.1. Improvement Science Dissertation in Practice (ISDiP) Journey Engaging the Literature

In this chapter, we turn to an essential part of all dissertations—the review of literature. We argue that the traditional PhD dissertation literature review does not serve practitioners, nor does it serve the dissertation in practice (DiP). We argue instead that reviewing the literature is a critical skill that practitioners need to know as part of their leadership toolbox. In the following chapter, we discuss how the literature can serve scholarly practitioners in framing problems of practice (PoPs), developing a theory of improvement, and framing the analysis of the data they gather during the improvement process.

Practitioners often enter EdD programs with 5–25 years of practical experience and knowledge. This age is in contrast to students, who often enter PhD programs directly out of their master's degree or after only a few years of practical experience. In traditional programs, practitioner knowledge and experience are often cast aside because faculty privilege academic research and knowledge over practical experience. However, as practitioners face growing challenges around equity, justice, and calls for accountability, faculty in schools of education have the responsibility to respond to practitioners' needs by preparing them with the skills they need to address the problems they face. Faculty members can no longer consider these students in the ways they have traditionally viewed doctoral students—as mentees or those who follow along under their tutelage studying the content area for which they are experts, nor can EdD students be treated "less than" PhD students, viewed merely as a revenue stream for schools of education. Faculty need to understand that educational practitioners have a broad range of knowledge and skills that have served them well over many years, but they want to know more because they have first-hand knowledge of the pressures and consequences of not addressing problems. Practitioners come to EdD programs in large numbers seeking to learn better skills for how to address the problems they face.

For many faculty members, teaching practitioners will require a shift in how they think about their programs and pedagogy by asking questions like, *Who are they preparing?* and, *What can they offer practitioners who are highly qualified at what they do?* The answer to the first question should be scholarly practitioners and the answer to the second should, in part, be access to, and understanding of, literature.

EdD students need literature because it is impossible for their faculty to be experts on each problem area students bring, especially when programs enroll from 25 to 100 students or more per year. However, practitioners do not necessarily need a heavy amount of literature around content knowledge because they are not going to be experts in a certain area or topic. EdD students needed balance and expansion. Practitioners don't typically have the expertise, understanding, and application of research to practice that faculty do (Lysenko, Abrami, Bernard, & Dagenais, 2015; Penuel, Farrell, Allen, Toyama, & Coburn, 2018; West & Rhoton, 1994). That is, traditionally practitioners are not trained to utilize literature and research to inform their understanding of problems, nor do they consult these tools as a means to improve their practice. What school of education faculty have the opportunity to do is bring their expertise and ability to engage scholarship and employ inquiry to understand and produce evidence about problems and potential solutions. The faculty role, therefore, is to expand EdD students' thinking about a problem and potential solutions by teaching them to use literature and theories and to prepare them to use research methods as tools to solve or improve problems.

Chapter 1 explained a backward mapping process for program design and noted the importance of literature in the DiP because it is used to frame the problem, develop a theory of improvement, and understand if the implemented intervention was an improvement. Given this important role, faculty must carefully consider where and how students will learn the skills of searching the literature, analyzing the validity and reliability of what they read, and building arguments and conceptual frameworks that support their understanding of a problem and potential solutions. Further, faculty must consider how practitioners will apply these skills in practice. If the DiP is meant to be a demonstration of how students have become scholarly practitioners, then it needs to engage literature in ways that are different than what happens in traditional five-chapter dissertations. The problems EdD students focus on are multi-dimensional, happen in daily practice, and often require multiple lenses to understand them: "Problem definition cannot be done by simply reviewing the extant literature [for a gap]" (Archbald, 2008, p. 716). Rather, the literature must broaden the student's thinking about their problem while situating it in a larger context. The literature also advances the student's thinking about potential solutions and determining if those solutions produced change.

The Purpose of a Literature Review

The literature review has been a constant part of dissertation work, though not often the most important part. In recent years, several scholars have sought to better define its role in the dissertation. For instance, in their seminal piece, Boote and Beile (2005) offer several purposes for the literature review. Reviewing the literature, they explain, allows the researcher to set the broad context of the study, situate existing literature in scholarly and historical context, report on claims, and examine research methods used to determine if claims are warranted with the ultimate goal of allowing the researcher to distinguished what has been done and what still needs to be learned (Boote & Beile, 2005). Lubke, Paulus, Britt, and Atkins (2017) have described this process as "synthesizing sources and writing an academic argument" (p. 289). Holley and Harris (2019) have explained that the literature review "serves as the vehicle for demonstrating the [student's] knowledge of research related to their dissertation" (p. 69). Many more have defined the literature review along these lines and have offered strategies for tackling the task of writing what often can be the hardest part of a traditional dissertation.

In the literature chapter of a PhD dissertation, a student documents what is known about their topic area, providing context and background that justify their research questions and the study they wish to undertake. They identify theories that frame their academic lens and develop conceptual frameworks that bring together existing literature to frame their particular study and situate the learning they will contribute to the field as a result. Further, the literature can provide the PhD student with justification for the methods they will use in their study and help them in interpreting their findings. The purpose and process of writing the PhD literature review are skills learned during a graduate program in preparation for entering the academic profession.

For the EdD student, in contrast, the review of literature cannot be an "uncritical canvassing of everything written on the subject" (*Harvard EdLD Handbook*, 2018) because not only is the extant literature massive and literally impossible to review in a reasonable timeframe, but also searching it for a "gap in theoretical knowledge" (Archbald, 2008) does not make sense for the practitioner who seeks to understand the complexities of organizational problems. Rather, in preparing professionals, the literature is a practical

Table 4.1. Comparison of Literature Use in PhD and EdD Dissertations

Traditional PhD Use of Literature	EdD Use of Literature
Set context of research study	Problem identification and rationalization
Situate in scholarly/historical contexts	Situate problem in broader context
Report on existing claims	Identify root causes of problem
Examine research methods	Develop conceptual framework/ theory of improvement
Identify a gap in knowledge	Build arguments for improvement
Demonstrate student understanding	Identify what field doesn't know
Frame researcher lens	Frame study of intervention or investigation
Justify research methodology	Serve as analytic starting point

tool that practitioners can add to their toolbox for improvement. It serves to increase insight about problems and contextualize those problems in what others have found about them. It also provides an empirical base of evidence for case building and solution proposition. In this sense, reviewing the literature becomes a critical skill that practitioners must learn in order to be impactful scholarly practitioners. Engaging literature in this way is exemplified at several EdD program around the United States. For example, at the University of Illinois at Chicago, EdD students studying educational leadership "draw upon relevant literature to provide a rationale for their focal areas of root cause problem identification [and] in the design of data collection tools" (Cosner, Tozer, & Zavitkovsky, 2016, p. 172). In the University of Florida Educational Technology EdD program, "relevant literature is used to rationalize the problem, frame the study and, when applicable, support design of interventions" (Dawson & Kumar, 2016, p. 135). Students in the Rutgers University interdisciplinary EdD program use literature to "understand the 'local' problem of practice within a broader context as a way to help them frame the problem, to inform their thinking about appropriate interventions, and as analytic starting points" (Belzer and Ryan, p. 203). These examples demonstrate a stark contrast to the PhD literature review and highlight the important role that literature plays in professional preparation. The literature is central to improving practice and is utilized throughout the DiP process.

What's in a name?

In addition to understanding the purpose of reviewing the literature, knowing what to call it is equally important. Many EdD programs continue to call this section of the DiP the "literature review" just as it is called in traditional doctoral dissertations. We argue, however, that language matters. Continuing to use terms that come from the traditional dissertation can lead students and faculty into a traditional mindset, circumventing the purpose of literature for practitioners and perpetuating the traditional purpose for the review of literature. As we have established above, the review fulfills very different purposes in professional preparation. Renaming what we call this exercise to reflect its role in EdD programs can shift faculty mindsets to the understanding that the literature is a tool, and reviewing it is a critical skill needed for professional practice. In some EdD programs, the name has shifted to reflect these different functions. For example, the Harvard Graduate School of Education Educational Leadership Program (EdLD) practitioner doctorate, refers to the review of literature as the "Review of Knowledge for Action (RKA)" (Harvard EdLD Handbook, 2018). This name implies the function of the review is to expand student understanding of a problem and to empower the student to act upon the problem. The University of Pittsburgh EdD program calls the exercise the "Review of Scholarly and Professional Knowledge," underscoring the notion that the review should go beyond academic literature to include literature from professional journals and giving students the full scope of how the problem has been identified and investigated.

Years ago, Shulman et al. (2006) proposed the idea of renaming the EdD. The authors offered the title of the *Professional Practice Doctorate* (PPD) to reframe the badly tarnished reputation of the degree. Though this title has not been taken on formally, the EdD is now commonly known as the professional practice doctorate in education. The authors claimed, however, that the name didn't matter as long as the degree components changed. Over the 13 years of the Carnegie Project on the Education Doctorate (CPED), much has changed about the EdD, including the purpose and the academic components that comprise this degree. Yet, despite the efforts of over 100 schools of education, distinguishing the EdD continues to be hampered because of the long and continued history of comparing it to the PhD. Lakoff (2004) advanced the idea that changing language is equally important to shifting beliefs and understanding. Therefore, we suggest that to truly distinguish the EdD as the professional practice doctorate, we need to shift the way we talk about degree and the components that comprise it, such as the DiP. As faculty develop the DiP for their program, they should change the purpose and name of the review of literature.

Literature as a Tool for Solving Problems of Practice

Literature that EdD students review should be both scholarly and practice based. Scholarly literature includes theories, existing knowledge, and empirical research. As faculty work to expand EdD students' thinking about problem solving, the scholarly literature should open their minds to new ideas, theories, and evidence related to their PoP. Theory in scholarly literature can broaden student thinking. However, theory is often difficult for practitioners to grasp. In blogging about the impact of theory on practitioner use of research evidence, Doucet (2019) explains that theory can offer practitioners three ways to think about and find solutions to educational problems. First, theory can provide a "richer conceptual understanding" of localized problems and offer "ideas about how to disrupt" the status quo (Doucet, 2019, p. 1). Established and tested theories provide foundations upon which best practices are built. Exposing students to theory opens avenues for thinking differently about their local context and about how they might improve it. Next, theory can "empower" a practitioner in the inquiry process.

As students learn to apply theory to practice, they move away from intuitive problem solving to what others have found through their work. Finally, theory can "advance an idea or set of actions meant to disrupt" the status quo (Doucet, 2019, p. 7). Theory provides evidence for building persuasive arguments for change. Introducing theory, however, needs to be done in ways that practitioners see its utility. Zambo & Zambo (2016) have argued that practitioners in EdD programs can be "blinded by their personal theories and resist [scholarly] theory if it fails to be persuasive, compelling, or relevant to their professional and research needs" (p. 20). They suggest when teaching theory faculty must "blend theories with professional and practical wisdom to allow scholarly practitioners to better understand, motivate and educate [within their organizations]" (p. 21). For instance, if teaching critical race theory to a group of EdD students, also teaching them how to apply this lens to decision making, parent and student expectations, or evaluating teaching to determine if the needs of all students and parents in their community are being met. This idea aligns with the CPED Framework, which explains that scholarly practitioners should have the abilities to use practical research and applied theories as tools for change.

Practice-based literature includes practitioner journals, professional association reports, and other learning that has been generated within a professional area. Noted in Shulman's (2007) definition of a profession (see Chapter 1), professions possess a growing body of knowledge, research, and practice as well as a mastery of technical skills and practices. This knowledge, often documented in professional journals and associations, supports the best practices of the practitioner's field and often is the basis for their professional ways of doing and being. This expertise cannot be discarded as it provides information about the realities of the field and the issue the student is investigating. Knowledge from practitioner and scholarly literature should be blended with what students know to generate intervention for improvement.

Literature in the ISDiP

In the ISDiP, the review of literature can serve three important purposes that are spread throughout the improvement journey. First, it supports the student in the naming and framing of a problem (understanding the problem). Next, it can aid the student in moving from their intuitive ideas toward a theory of change (developing a theory of improvement). Finally, the literature can serve to situate findings or results from interventions (testing a change). Figure 4.2 offers a visual of these steps.

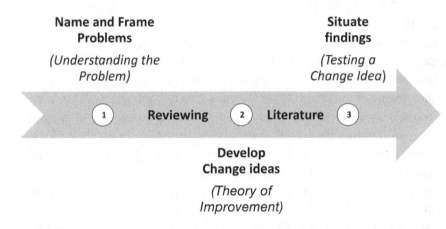

Figure 4.2. Steps of the DiP Where Literature Serves a Purpose

The first step of the improvement journey is understanding the problem. Students generate fishbones to find the root causes of their problem and do empathy interviews and observations to understand how others view the problem. Employing literature as a tool advances a student's understanding by situating their problem into a broader context, one that demonstrates that the problem is rooted in larger "universal" issues rather than being a "unique" and localized problem (Hochbein & Perry, 2013). Belzer and Ryan (2013) further explain that the literature "contextualizes [a problem] within big ideas that may bring the problem into sharper focus, identify root causes of the problem, and help etch out appropriate entry points for investigation that truly have the potential to help solve the problem" (pp. 203–204).

As a tool, the literature adds to the student's practical understanding by "provid[ing] supporting evidence for a practical problem or issue which [the student's] research is addressing" (Ridley, 2012, p. 24). Through the review, the EdD student learns how their problem has been framed in different ways and in different contexts. Additionally, the review can help shape the student's understanding about what the field does and does not know about the problem and where their learning might contribute to this understanding.

Archbald (2008) describes the process of utilizing the literature in this way as "building a case for a problem" (p. 716) to convince others that the problem exists and that it is urgent enough that it warrants improving. In an ISDiP, literature plays an important role. Therefore, it should be introduced early in the program and the improvement journey. Doing so will serve two purposes. First, it will broaden student thinking and support their ability to accurately name and frame their PoP. Second, knowing that students will continue to read as their program continues deepens their understanding of the importance of this critical skill.

The second step comes as students continue down the improvement journey. The literature can support the student in developing a theory of improvement by learning what has been done to understand and solve the problem. Mintrop (2016) notes that literature has the powerful purpose of moving a practitioner from their intuitive ideas towards action by helping them link ideas between practice and literature. Students build upon their practitioner's intuition to create "actionable knowledge," or knowledge that "can support practicable action in specific organizational contexts" (Argyris, 1990). Belzer and Ryan (2013), refer to reviewing the literature to create a rationale for "making intervention decisions to solve gaps in practice" (p. 203). They explain that students

> are not making up [solutions] out of the blue or inventing the wheel over and over again in deciding what to do to solve a problem. Rather, they are turning to the literature for research-based solutions and testing them out to see how they work in local contexts with particular conditions on the ground. (p. 203)

Here, we see the literature again being used as a tool. Reviewing how a problem has been researched and the empirical evidence that describes the impact of the problem and potential solutions provides fodder for a student's own thinking about how to address the problem locally.

Teaching practitioners how to search for and employ literature in the naming and framing of problems and the development of a theory of improvement moves them away from the place many begin their EdD program—offering a solution without really understanding what the problem is. Bryk, et al. (2015) call this "solutionitis." Those of us who have worked with EdD students know that many are anxious to enact solutions without having a firm understanding of the problem or its roots. Teaching practitioners to engage the literature in these ways not only eliminates solutionitis, but it also gives them specific, transferrable skills to use research and literature to define future problems, interventions, and measures.

The third step happens once students have implemented their intervention and gathered data. They will need a starting point upon which to begin their analysis. The literature can serve this purpose in several ways. It might provide initial codes for coding qualitative data. It might situate findings or results from interventions into a broader perspective. Or it might provide a basis for comparison of result to other studies of the problem.

Reviewing as a Skill

With most EdD students returning to schools at later ages, chances are they have not searched for or conducted any kind of research in many years, if ever. Teaching these practitioners how to search and utilize the literature is imperative. Firestone, Perry, Leland and McKeon (2019) emphasize this point. In their work, they find that before learning to use evidence in practice, educational practitioners need to be taught "how to find and organize it, how to understand it, how to assess it, how to identify a problem that could be studied, and how to conduct research (Firestone et al., 2019, p. 8). The EdD course work and exercises, they explain, must teach the skill of reviewing the literature. Though this skill may seem similar to what PhD students do, it is different because the purpose of the literature review is different. Students in EdD programs need to be taught to:

- search for literature in online databases;
- read literature in both simplified and detailed manners;
- assess the validity of articles they read;
- understand the contributions and limitations of research studies;
- compare and contrast findings;
- organize bibliographies of usable knowledge;
- synthesize to frame PoPs; and
- communicate their insights to other constituencies (Firestone et al., 2019; Hochbein & Perry, 2013).

Additionally, teaching the skill of reviewing literature is one that should be taught as a professional skill, not an academic skill. As scholarly practitioners, students in EdD programs should continue to return to literature as they encounter new problems. Therefore, reviewing the literature needs to be taught in a way that doesn't consume students with skills they will not use in practice (e.g., reviewing large amounts of literature to find a gap). It must be taught systematically and practically. Firestone et al. (2019) have also discovered that many alumni of EdD programs find reviewing literature to be useful for practice, yet upon graduation, they lose access to their university libraries and cannot afford to purchase access articles. If we expect scholarly practitioners to utilize research evidence from literature in their practice, we need to make literature available. We encourage faculty to work with their library systems to ensure this access is available for their graduates as a means to support their work as scholarly practitioners.

Because the literature review has been treated the same for both PhD and EdD students, little has been written about how EdD students should go about reviewing the literature. Mintrop (2016) has provided the clearest explanation of how practitioners should review the literature to inform PoP definition and intervention design. In his book, *Design-Based School Improvement: A Practical Guide for*

Education Leaders, he explains that though practitioners do not need to have "full command of published research studies and professional wisdom," they do need to have their "intuitive assumptions justified by what the knowledge base suggests" (p. 77). He describes the process of reviewing as searching for, organizing, and using literature to frame problems and design interventions. In searching the literature, practitioners can begin with their intuitive ideas and hunches to create search terms. They then select a database to search. While ERIC, Google Scholar, and Web of Science are common places to search, faculty should encourage practitioners to also consider dissertation databases, such as PROQUEST, which offer a broad range of pieces by doctoral students that are frequently not turned into research articles. As students search these databases, they should determine if sources are useful by looking at the number of citations to determine the credibility of the work; reviewing the title, abstract, and key words to determine if the article is worth reading fully; looking at specific authors or the date of publication to determine if the sources is useful; and reviewing the bibliography or references to find other sources to investigate.

The literature is a tool and should be engaged as such. Students might do a specific search where they look for a "narrow fit" (Mintrop, 2016, p. 80) between the literature and their initial thinking about a PoP. Specific searches might provide key terms that students can then use in their search. More often than not, students will probably do a general search and find a "broader area of knowledge" that offers "concepts, findings, or controversies in the field" (Mintrop, 2016, p. 80). Mintrop (2016) also suggests that students look outside of the field of education literature. Fields such as sociology, economics, and psychology may offer very different views about certain problems or areas in education.

Once sources have been compiled, they need to be organized for review. Utilizing a citation management system, such as EndNote or Mendeley, will not only help students manage the numerous sources they gather, but it will also help them to employ American Psychological Association (APA) style in their writing. Mintrop (2016) suggests a first step to organization be to group sources by genre (e.g., theoretical, empirical, reviews of knowledge, practitioner knowledge) to distinguish between the peer-reviewed research base and practitioner wisdom, which will be important when utilizing these sources in the ISDiP. After creating these groups, he suggests next looking at the "findings, conclusions and suggested recommendations" across all of the sources (Mintrop, 2016, p. 82) so the student can build what he calls a "robust knowledge base" for understanding (p. 82). A robust knowledge base, he notes:

- is based on established and widely accepted theories;
- is based in a good number of strong empirical studies;
- condenses multiple empirical studies;
- differs in methods, both in-depth interpretations of qualitative data and generalizations through statistical analysis of quantitative data; and
- provides solid reporting on practical applications of research (Mintrop, 2016, p. 82).

From this robust knowledge base, Mintrop (2016) tells students to look for consistency around the problem by asking, "What behavioral patterns (beliefs, attitudes, practices) do the sources report? Are these patterns consistent or inconsistent across sources? If inconsistent why?" (p. 83). Students may find consistency around definitions, types of methods utilized, and findings. Alternatively, they may find that their sources are inconsistent, signifying the "whole field of research about a given topic may be plagued with rival empirical methods, explanations, and theories," which, Mintrop (2016) explains, is "not unusual in social research" (p. 83). Either way, students begin to situate their problem by identifying how it is defined and framed in the literature, and what has been done to address the problem in various contexts.

Next, students utilize the literature in their ISDiP to identify and contextualize PoPs, build a case for potential solutions, and support their analysis and interpretation of intervention results. Mintrop (2016) observes that the professional and research base is often "not comprehensive enough" around specific problems and instead, the student may need to "stitch together" the knowledge to build their arguments (p. 84). We explain this as creating understanding through building a conceptual framework. Students use the review of literature exercise to organize bodies of scholarly and professional literature to frame an understanding about the broader issue in which their PoP is situated as well as the local PoP. The review is their opportunity to explain what they have learned from these bodies of literature and reinforce their argument that the problem is an actionable one requiring that a specific change take place. Kumar and Antonenko (2014) have defined a conceptual framework in EdD programs as "a system of assumptions, expectations, beliefs, theories, and concepts that support and inform research" (p. 55). For the practitioners they teach at the University of Florida, conceptual frameworks help to align and guide DiPs by giving the student a larger view of how their intuitive thinking, the professional knowledge, and the scholarly literature come together to formulate their own thinking about the problem and its potential solution. The conceptual framework will contribute to the fishbone diagram and defining the root causes of the problem. The fishbone is fluid and constantly changing as the student learns more about their problem. Therefore, students should return to their initial fishbone diagram and add the knowledge they have gained from reviewing the scholarly and professional literature.

The conceptual framework will help students identify a theory of improvement by providing evidence for potential solutions. By visualizing their system of thinking, students can begin to identify potential solutions that are grounded in evidence-based knowledge. It will also be a place where students return when they analyze the results from their interventions. The conceptual framework will continue to be a work in progress throughout the ISDiP process as students continue to gather more knowledge. Below is an example of a conceptual framework for an EdD student (Silvi) studying higher education administration. She is seeking to determine why the mentors in her professional physician assistant (PA) program are not effective in mentoring PA candidates.

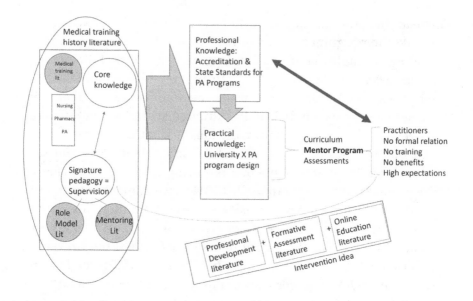

Figure 4.3. Sample Conceptual Framework

As scholarly practitioners in professional settings, conceptual frameworks that bring together evidence and organizational data that is grounded in the literature can "persuade others of a gap between an existing state in an organization and a preferred state, and for building a case for change—not just change but improvement" (Archbald, 2008, pp. 715–716). Viewing literature as a tool and learning the important ability to apply this tool to practice is "a distinguishing feature between how a professional practice doctoral student approaches a problem of practice and how a typical practitioner might" (Dawson & Kumar, 2016, p. 135).

A note about group dissertations: Group dissertations are become more common across EdD programs as faculty recognize that practitioners do not work in isolation. In their everyday roles, they problem solve in teams or with peers. Many forms of the group dissertation exist and the topic is worthy of its own book. For our purposes, however, if your students are working in a group on their DiP, the review of literature is a key place where they can easily collaborate. Together, they can search extensively across the scholarly and professional literature to build a rich conceptual framework while learning the value of working collaboratively in problem defining.

EdD programs educate professionals to become scholarly practitioners, which means literature plays a very central role in this training process. As a tool, the literature gives practitioners who face daily problems a large and rich base for understanding problems and developing effective solutions. Many students tell us about the eye-opening experiences they have had as they learn that the issues they face have been studied deeply. As a skill, it shapes the improvement science research process—identifying a problem, developing a theory of improvement, and analyzing intervention results. The literature also shapes thinking by supporting students in moving from intuition to evidence-based practice.

Summary

This chapter reframes thinking around the purpose and role of reviewing the literature in a DiP. Literature is described as a tool for practitioners to use in problem solving, both in their dissertation work and, more importantly, in their professional practice. Reviewing both the scholarly and professional knowledge is a critical skill, and scholarly practitioners need to learn how to best utilize this tool. We describe the distinct purposes that the literature serves in the DiP—to name and frame a problem, to support the development of a theory of improvement, and to provide an initial framework for analysis.

Post-reading questions for faculty

1. How does your EdD program view the review of literature in the DiP?
2. How are your students taught to review literature as scholarly practitioners distinct from the way your PhD students are taught?
3. Does your library allow alumni to access its databases? If not, how might you change that policy?

Post-reading questions for scholarly practitioners/students

1. How do you perceive this new vision of the review of literature? Do you find it useful to both your program and your practice?
2. How might you go about developing a conceptual framework that visually supports your thinking about your PoP?
3. How might you share what you have learned in the literature with your professional colleagues?

References

Archbald, D. (2008). Research versus problem solving for education leadership doctoral thesis: Implications for form and function. *Educational Administration Quarterly, 44*(5), 704–739.

Argyris, C. (1990). *Overcoming organizational defenses: Facilitating organizational learning*. Boston, MA: Allyn and Bacon.

Belzer, A. & Ryan, S. (2013). Defining the problem of practice dissertation: Where's the Practice, What's the Problem? *Planning and Changing, 44*(3/4), pp 195–207.

Boote, D. & Beile, P. (2005). Scholars before researchers: On the centrality of the dissertation literature review in research preparation. *Educational Researcher. 34*(6). pp. 3–15.

Bryk, A.S., Gomez, L.M., Gunrow, A., & LeMahieu, P.G. (2015). Breaking the cycle of failed school reforms: Using network improvement communities to learn fast and implement well. *Harvard Education Letter, 31*(1), 1–3.

Cosner, S., Tozer, S., & Zavitkovsky, P. (2016). Enacting a cycle of inquiry capstone research project in doctoral-level leadership preparation. In *Contemporary approaches to dissertation development and research methods* (pp. 162–183). Hershey, PA: IGI Global.

Dawson, K. & Kumar S. (2016). Guiding principles for quality professional practice dissertations. In V.A. Storey & K.A. Hesbol (Eds.), Contemporary approaches to dissertation development and research methods (pp. 133–146). Hershey, PA: Information Science Reference.

Doucet, F. (2019). Centering the margins: (Re)defining useful research evidence through critical perspectives. New York: William T. Grant Foundation.

Firestone, W.A., Perry, J.A., Leland, A.S., & McKeon, R.T. (2019). Teaching research and data use in the education doctorate. *Journal of Research on Leadership Education.* https://doi.org/10.1177/1942775119872231

Harvard Graduate School of Education. (2018). EdLD Handbook.

Hochbein, C. & Perry, J.A. (2013) The role of research in the professional doctorate. *Planning and Changing, 44*(3/4), 181–194.

Holley, K. & Harris, M. (2019). The qualitative dissertation in education: A guide for integrating research and practice. New York:Routledge

Kumar, S., & Antonenko, P. (2014). Connecting practice, theory and method: Supporting professional doctoral students in developing conceptual frameworks. *TechTrends, 58*(4), 54–61.

Lakoff, G. (2004). Don't think of an elephant: Know your values and frame the debate. White River Junction, VT: Chelsea Green Publishing.

Lubke, J., Paulus, T.M., Britt, V.G., & Atkins, D.P. (2017). Hacking the literature review: Opportunities and innovations to improve the research process. *Reference & User Services Quarterly, 56*(4), 285–295.

Lysenko, L., Abrami, P., Bernard, R., & Dagenais, C. (2015). Research use in education: An online survey of school practitioners. *Brock Education Journal, 25*(1), 35–54.

Mintrop, R. (2016). *Design-based school improvement: A practical guide for education leaders.* Cambridge, MA: Harvard Education Press.

Penuel, W.R., Farrell, C.C., Allen, A.-R., Toyama, Y., & Coburn, C.E. (2018). What research district leaders find useful. *Educational Policy, 32*(4), 540–568.

Ridley, D. (2012). *The literature review: A step-by-step guide for students.* Thousand Oaks, CA:Sage.

Shulman, L.S. (2007). *Scholarships of practice and the practice of scholarship: Education among the doctorates.* Paper presented at the Council of Graduate Schools.

Shulman, L.S., Golde, C.M., Bueschel, A.C., & Garabedian, K.J. (2006). Reclaiming education's doctorates: A critique and a proposal. *Educational researcher, 35*(3), 25–32.

West, R.F., & Rhoton, C. (1994). School district administrators' perceptions of educational research and barriers to research utilization. *ERS Spectrum, 12*(1), 23–30.

Zambo, D., & Zambo, R. (2016). The role of theory in EdD programs and dissertations in practice. In *Contemporary approaches to dissertation development and research methods* (pp. 17–28). Hershey, PA:IGI Global.

CHAPTER FIVE

Driver Diagrams and a Theory of Improvement

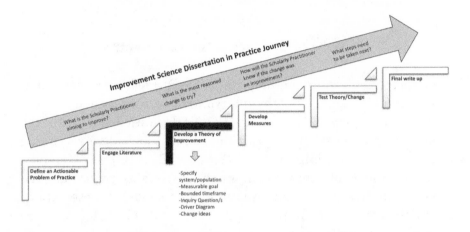

Figure 5.1. Improvement Science Dissertation in Practice Journey Developing a Theory of Improvement

> Rational prediction requires theory and builds knowledge through systematic revision and extension of theory based on comparison of prediction with observation. (Deming, 1993, p. 69)

The previous chapters have provided a discussion on the process of establishing a problem of practice (PoP) and using the causal systems analysis technique to diagram the underlying root causes of PoPs. This chapter builds on that learning and helps scholarly practitioners doing an Improvement Science Dissertation in Practice (ISDiP) know how to establish a theory of improvement and hypothesize potential actions that might lead to an improvement. Formulating a theory of improvement is important for educational leaders because they need to know how to remedy the PoP that they face. The tools of improvement science can help leaders understand their problems' causes so that they can then be redirected and mapped on to areas for targeted change. This chapter provides information on how to use a driver diagram as a means for determining a theory of improvement as well as a source for generating potential data for measuring attempts at improvements.

What Is a Theory of Improvement?

As the ISDiP journey continues, work performed in problem identification (fishbone, empathy interviews, and process and systems maps) and review of scholarly and practical knowledge moves to the point where the scholarly practitioner must articulate a working theory of practice improvement (Bryk, et al., 2015). Developing a working theory of improvement is neither straightforward nor obvious. It requires that a scholarly practitioner blend their observations with the literature and with their own practical knowledge. A theory of improvement is an explicit statement that responds to the question, *"What will work to improve the problem?"* More specifically, a theory of improvement is a group's best thinking at the time about "articulat[ing] a hypothesis, outlining exactly how you see changes in practice sparking improvement" (New York City Department of Education, 2018, p. 43). Further, a theory of improvement describes how the scholarly practitioner will move from problem analysis to actually tackling the problem during the testing phase.

It is necessary to articulate a theory of improvement prior to moving into action. Note that when developing a theory of improvement, the scholarly practitioner must consider both the larger goals for the project (*Where are areas of influence that might "move the needle" on improving the overall aim?*) as well as smaller goals that focus on the individual events and actions which, taken as a whole, form the constellation of change ideas believed to increase the outcomes sought. Both large and small goals not only play an important part in providing an overall focus for the work, but they also serve as the catalyst spurring the articulation of the individual actions which, taken in tandem, are responsible for "moving the needle" in relation to achieving their associated outcomes (Marshall, Pronovost, & Dixon-Woods, 2013). This work requires one to "develop the theoretical base for the study of improvement, including organizational, innovation, social and behavioral theories, as well as the mechanisms of change associated with ... the modes of improvement" (p. 343).

A theory of improvement articulates "testable predictions of the activities and infrastructure necessary to achieve a desired outcome" (Bennett & Provost, 2015, p. 38). Therefore, developing the theory becomes a key step in the process of hypothesizing about the changes that, once implemented, will ultimately lead to achieving the improvement aim. Creating the theory of improvement is a collaborative endeavor, done by crafting and refining with input from relevant stakeholders.

Getting from the what to the how: The driver diagram

In Chapter 3, root causes determined to be responsible for a problem's existence can be derived through the process of constructing a fishbone diagram. Now, at this point in the ISDiP journey, the scholarly practitioner must focus on translating each (or most) of the major causal factors into proactive elements, which, if addressed independently, might be a means for improvement. Moving to concrete thinking about specific changes that might rectify a problem of practice is attained by employing another improvement tool, *the driver diagram.*

A driver diagram is an improvement tool that aids the scholarly practitioner in several ways (note Figure 5.2). The diagram is used to organize the group's best ideas at the time. The diagram shows leverage points in a system where change might happen. The diagram provides a graphic for "visually representing a group's working theory of practice improvement" (Bryk, et al., 2015, p. 199) and allows the scholarly practitioner to test the working hypothesis or prediction about *"What might work?"* [emphasis added] (Bennett & Provost, 2015). The diagram permits the identification of major elements, which, if changes were introduced within a system, could

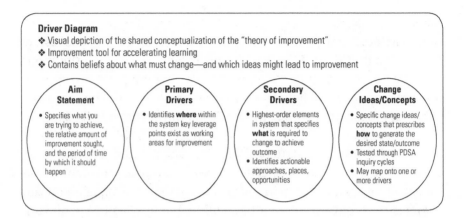

Figure 5.2. Overview of the Driver Diagram

allow for the description of positive effects as contributing toward the improvement aim. For the ISDiP, the driver diagram "illustrates what structures, processes and norms are believed to require change in the system, as well as how these could be changed through the application of specific ideas" (Bennett & Provost, 2015, p. 39). As a whole, the identification and selection of one or more changes puts the scholarly practitioner well on the way to improving system elements that could potentially lead to positively impacting the overall improvement aim. It is important to note that the driver diagram represents the "big picture" of the many potential avenues (i.e., key drivers) of improvement. In the ISDiP, if the project is to be undertaken individually, a single high-leverage driver may be the focus of the work. However, if the dissertation in practice is to be undertaken collectively as a group, then more than a single key driver may be targeted based on the increased human resource capacity to widen the scope of the work.

What are the components of the driver diagram?

Read from left to right, the driver diagram begins with the aim statement. The aim statement specifies precisely what the improvement initiative hopes to achieve. For example, noted in Figure 5.3

below, the aim statement is to "increase the district graduation rate by 20% by the end of the school year." The statement is written in a way that defines the parameters of the improvement effort: how much is expected? (a 20% increase); for whom is this supposed to happen? (district students); and by when is it supposed to occur? (end of the school year). On a driver diagram, "Everything to the right-hand side of the aim statement identifies a theory about what must change and how it must change to achieve the desired performance or outcome" (Bennett & Provost, 2015, p. 39).

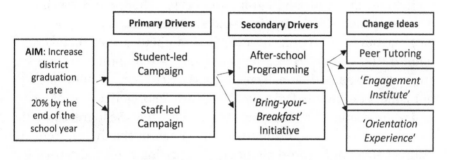

Figure 5.3. Example of a Driver Diagram

The aim statement is written clearly and explicitly, meaning that the statement is crafted to be specific, measurable, aspirational, relevant, and time-bound, and it answers the question, *"What are we trying to accomplish?"* The aim statement describes both the specific problem to be solved and the measure of the amount of change expected. In crafting the aim statement, it is imperative that the statement specify 1) what the goal is, 2) the timeframe within which the goal should be met, and 3) a measurement (score, result, etc.) to be used for evaluating progress toward attaining the desired goal (Bryk, et al., 2015).

Given that an ISDiP is a complex, time-bound endeavor, the aim should reflect a narrowing of the scope of the work to be completed. Primary reasons for narrowing the scope of the project are feasibility in completion, the potential to leverage resources, and the nature of the task. Further, regarding scope, one must consider the extent to which one individual completing the ISDiP has the capacity to undertake. Questions one might ask at this stage in the process include: *What expert knowledge do I have? What can I procure for guiding this work?* and *What resources are available?* In evaluating the answers to these questions, a realistic aim can be formulated. Further, aims may vary as the change effort progresses. They are not necessarily static as it is typical for the aims to be refined based on the generation of and reflection on new learning.

As the diagram is read from left to right, the second column contains the primary drivers. In our example about an ISDiP focused on increasing the district's graduation rates, there are two primary drivers: student-led campaigns and staff-led campaigns. The campaigns, therefore, represent a prediction about a specific leverage point in the system. Here, the campaigns are designed to increase student engagement and, by proxy, serve to influence achieving the outcome: graduation. Primary drivers are an organized set of ideas, and when changes are introduced and measured, the increase would signal the change as an improvement. Each of the drivers reflects a direct inverse of those elements comprising the root causes for the problem. For example, if it is found during a root cause analysis that lack of student engagement is a contributing causal factor for declining graduation rates, conversely, in the driver diagram, the finding would be mapped on to a driver diagram, introducing a proactive strategy aimed at increasing student engagement. Note Figure 5.3.

Driver diagrams allow a scholarly practitioner to devise a theory of improvement that guides the next step's action. Once primary drivers are identified, the process continues wherein each primary driver is broken down into its component parts: the secondary drivers. As depicted in Figure 5.3, the primary driver of a student-led campaign can further be broken down into discrete parts representing the secondary drivers, which become more granular from left to right as one reads across the driver diagram. Considering the figure, the secondary drivers represent those elements that can be made actionable, such as creating after-school programming to increase student engagement. Although the secondary drivers can grow to be an exhaustive list, attention should be paid to constraining the possible elements to those drivers over which the scholarly practitioner has the most leverage as well as drivers that have the potential to be the most impactful for spurring positive change. Carefully-chosen secondary drivers, such as after-school programming, are targeted actions for the outcomes desired in the improvement effort. Because of the breakdown, the secondary drivers provide more granularity and detail specific to the particular strategies that will be undertaken in order to "move the needle" towards achieving the aim. In our example, the primary driver of student-led campaigns to increase student engagement (and, by proxy, student retention) has two associated secondary drivers. It is common in breaking down a primary driver to arrive at more than one associated secondary driver.

The final piece of the diagram comprises the change ideas. A change idea is an "alteration to a system or process that is to be tested through a Plan-Do-Study-Act (PDSA) cycle, to examine its efficacy in improving some driver in the working theory of improvement" (Bryk, et al., 2015, p. 199). Change ideas are the most granular of the elements depicted and positioned in the right-most column in the driver diagram. As illustrated in Figure 5.3, it is common for several change ideas, possibly as many as three or four, to be linked to a secondary driver. In our example, after-school programming (secondary driver) is deconstructed further into the more granular change ideas of peer-tutoring, a student engagement "institute," and an orientation program.

Change ideas can be derived by consulting the literature. Empirical studies, particularly those focused on describing successful innovation and intervention, can provide a solid picture as the practitioner scholar uncovers elements proven, through rigorous testing and review, to work under certain conditions, for certain populations, and in certain contexts. Further, ideas for widening the collaboration might include conducting focus groups with students and others to get their views on how to solve the problem or for establishing a record for how students see themselves as being a part of the solution to increase fellow graduates. Taken together, change ideas arising through a review of literature for action and knowledge, as well as through consulting relevant stakeholders, can play a helpful role in informing the developing theory of improvement.

Typically, one to three change ideas will be associated with each secondary driver. In addition to being linked to secondary drivers, depending on the nature of the initiative, change ideas might also be connected to a group of measures. From our example, peer tutoring is a change idea that could be initiated as part of an improvement project. As such, a variety of process-related improvement questions apply: *How is the peer mentoring working? For whom?* and *Under what conditions?* As the most concrete of the driver diagram elements, the change ideas represent the *What?* that in which one wants to see improvements that are necessary for achieving the aim. Each change idea should have at least one corresponding PDSA inquiry cycle. For example, if there are three change ideas associated with a particular secondary driver (such as peer tutoring, an engagement institute, and an orientation experience), then each of these three introductions should have an associated PDSA inquiry cycle. We will discuss testing change ideas with our version of the inquiry cycle in Chapter 7.

Once one has compiled a list of change ideas, how does one decide upon which to enact? The answer to the question involves several considerations. To help decide upon which change ideas to include in the ISDiP, ask the following questions:

- Which change idea could produce the:
  - greatest impact?
  - most immediate return?
  - most value by the institution? and
  - most excitement with working?

Lastly, take into account whether the ISDiP will be tackled individually—or as a group. The scale and magnitude of the project, needless to say, should be weighed when deciding upon the course or courses of action.

Deciding upon drivers

A question to ask as a driver diagram is being constructed is, *Are the elements in the primary driver column sufficient for reaching the aim?* Elements in the primary driver column represent the *Where?* question. That is, where are there specific areas associated with the PoP that have the potential to leverage change? In our example, the two primary drivers provided, student-led campaigns and campaigns led by staff, represent categories where efforts made towards improvements might "move the needle" in attaining the ultimate aim: higher graduation rates. Increasing graduation rates for a school district might require additional primary drivers beyond solely student- and staff-led campaigns. A change effort might also involve parents or other relevant stakeholder groups in addition to efforts led by only those located in the school.

The ISDiP and driver diagrams

In the ISDiP, the construction of the driver diagram should be collaborative in nature and involve those most affected by the problem. For instance, the information gleaned from prior work in constructing the fishbone diagram (i.e., determining the causal factors contributing to the problem existence) is mapped on to the driver diagram, representing proactive elements that, if undertaken or enacted upon, might contribute positively toward attaining the aim.

Diagramming the drivers, or leverage points where change can lead to increases in improvement, has several benefits as a ubiquitous feature of the ISDiP. First, the driver diagram allows the practitioner and stakeholders to collaboratively identify the major spheres of influence where changes could be implemented. The primary drivers may be arranged by priority, chronology, or other ways based on contextual needs and demands. For example, two of the four primary drivers in a diagram align with both the school's annual improvement plan as well as the district's strategic initiative. It would make sense in this case, depending on the length of time for the project, the resources allocated, etc., to prioritize the drivers to those that are already perceived to be relevant and valued by school and district personnel.

Second, constructing the driver diagram, particularly if done collaboratively, allows stakeholders to granularize specific actions within each primary driver category. When each primary driver is broken down into its sub-component parts relevant to the overall category, these sub-components represent the secondary drivers. This helps the scholarly practitioner develop dissertation work that matters to their context.

A final benefit to constructing the driver diagram is that it becomes a roadmap for action. Looking at the driver diagram from right to left, we see a backward mapping, where each change idea is associated with a specific secondary driver, and each secondary driver is associated with a primary driver. In later chapters, we explain how each of the change ideas connected to secondary drivers can be parlayed into an improvement inquiry cycle and analyzed for new learning. For the ISDiP, this means having a roadmap and completing the dissertation on time. For complex projects typical of doctoral-level ISDiP work, the driver diagram contains a measurable aim statement, primary and secondary drivers, and associated change ideas connected to the secondary drivers. When interpreting a driver diagram, it is helpful to identify each necessary element by completing the blanks in the following sentence: "If we want to accomplish __[aim]__ we must __[primary driver]__ through/by/with __[secondary driver]_ and one way to do that is _[change idea]_ " (New York City Department of Education, 2018). From our earlier example, if a scholarly practitioner is tackling the problem of declining graduation rates, the district may work to improve on-time graduation, whereby their aim statement reads: "By the end of the school year, Southern Concordia School District will increase the graduation rate by 20%." Taken further, incorporating both the aim statement along with other components noted in the sentence above, the sentence would read, "If we want to increase Southern Concordia School District's graduation rate 20% by the end of the school year, we will hold a student-led campaign through which a sense of engagement will be fostered in the school community; and one way to do this is to support struggling students through a <u>one-to-one peer tutoring initiative</u>." From the information contained in the sentence, a path forward for the improvement initiative may be forged.

Summary

After causal elements have been identified, the next step in the ISDiP is to map these elements on to actionable change ideas. This chapter takes the reader into a discussion on the importance of and strategies for establishing a theory of improvement. Further, the reader is briefed on how, using causal analysis, the fishbone diagram yields information that is used as a basis for informing the development of the driver diagram. Lastly, we explain how the driver diagram organizes and prioritizes actions and where, if changes are made, increases seen would signal "moving the needle" towards the improvement aim.

Post-reading questions for faculty

1. How might you use a student's laboratory of practice as a context for generating data for informing a (developing) theory of improvement?
2. What types of examples might you draw upon as a way of illustrating the difference between primary drivers, secondary drivers, and change ideas?

Post-reading questions for scholarly practitioners/students

1. How might you collaboratively construct a theory of improvement? An aim statement?
2. In an improvement project, explain how information contained in a fishbone diagram informs the development of the driver diagram.
3. How might you determine whether a set of primary drivers are valued by members of the institution?

4. How might you decide upon the number and prioritization of a set of change ideas to include in a ISDiP?

References

Bennett, B., & Provost, L. (2015). What's your theory? Driver diagram serves as tool for building and testing theories for improvement. *Quality Progress, 48*(7), 36–43.

Bryk, A., Gomez, L., Grunow, A., & LeMahieu, P. (2015). *Learning to improve: How America's schools can get better at getting better.* Cambridge, MA: Harvard University Press.

Carnegie Foundation for the Advancement of Teaching. (2020). *Aim statements.* https://carnegienetworks.zendesk.com/hc/en-us/articles/115001233728-Aim-Statements

Deming, W.E. (1993). *The new economics for industry, government, education.* Cambridge, MA: MIT Press.

Langley, G., Moen, R., Nolan, K., Nolan, T., Norman, C., & Provost, L. (2009). *The improvement guide: A practical approach to enhancing organizational performance* (2nd ed.). San Francisco, CA: Jossey-Bass.

Marshall, M., Pronovost, P., & Dixon-Woods, M. (2013). Promotion of improvement as a science. *Lancet, 381*(9864), 419–421.

New York City Department of Education.(2018). *Improvement science handbook.* https://www.weteachnyc.org/media2016/filer_public/4b/40/4b4027b3-c0a6-4129-a050-7c41120a38d7/nycdoe_improvement_science_handbook_2018_online.pdf

Portela, M., Pronovost, P., Woodcock, T., Carter, P., & Dixon-Woods, M. (2015). How to study improvement interventions: A brief overview of possible study types. *BMJ Quality & Safety, 24*, 325–336.

CHAPTER SIX

Developing Improvement Measures

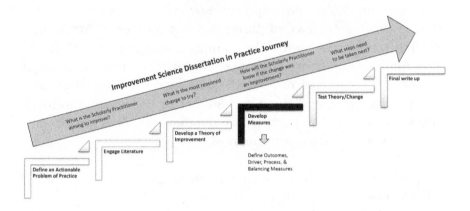

Figure 6.1. Improvement Science Dissertation in Practice (ISDiP) Journey Developing Measures

> Sound measurement tests our efforts to see whether they are improvements and provide evidence of impact and effects. (LeMahieu, et al., 2015, p. 447)

What Are Measures?

If written correctly, the ISDiP aim statement should provide very clear direction about where the improvement inquiry is heading. But how will a scholarly practitioner know if they have reached their aim? In improvement science, practical measurement is used to answer the question, *How will I know if the change was an improvement?* Practical measurement is unlike other forms of measurement. For example, measurement for research seeks to create new knowledge without paying particular attention to its applicability to practice. It quantifies latent variables and makes causal claims and predictions. Additionally, measurement for research can involve several instruments and take a long time to complete. Measurement for accountability, another example, seeks to determine choice, develop comparisons, or create a basis for change (Hinnant-Crawford, 2019; Solberg, Mosser, & McDonald, 1997). It is generally high-stakes, summative in nature, and comes after impact of an effort has happened. Practical measurement, in contrast, is comprised of limited, quick, and easy-to-collect data that provides information about whether or not an improvement effort is working. The Carnegie Foundation describes the characteristics of practical measurement as:

- producing data accessible in a timely manner;
- informing subsequent action;
- embedded in social routines that secure the trust and openness necessary to sustain meaningful change efforts;
- operationalizing the working theory;
- specific to the processes and outcomes needing to change;
- sensitive to change;
- predictive of outcomes; and
- having language meaningful to those engaged in the work (MichiganX, 2017).

Solberg, et al. (1997) describes three roles that measurement has in improvement work. First, measurement can serve to "better understand the extent and nature of the problem" (p. 139). Data are gathered to understand the system and define the problem phases of improvement. Examples of data for these purposes include empathy interviews, systems mapping and process mapping, and examining existing documentation. These data provide a baseline measure of understanding.

Second, measurement can serve to "provide motivation to change by documenting the extent of the problem" (Solberg, et al., 1997, p. 139). In their practice, as well as in their dissertation in practice (DiP), scholarly practitioners need measurement to build arguments supporting the claim that their problem of practice (PoP) truly is a problem in need of improvement. Such data-based arguments can lead to the momentum needed for improvement to happen across an organization. Data gathered from organizational documentation, scholarly and professional knowledge, and a series of empathy interviews and systems and process mapping all provide evidence of the problem and the extent to which it is affecting the system. As a leader, this improvement skill is extremely important. Learning to turn data into evidence upon which the leader can build claims and arguments and get others behind them are skills of becoming a scholarly practitioner.

Third, measurement can serve to "provide points of comparison with remeasurements obtained after changes are made" (Solberg, et al., 1997, p. 139). That is, measurement can provide baseline data for comparison to see if the change is working and how those impacted by the change feel about it. In the ISDiP, this third aspect of measurement happens during the implementation of the change idea. As you can see, practical measurement is embedded throughout the improvement process and is tied closely to the local context, local processes, and local people.

Measures in Improvement Science

As a multi-staged inquiry process, improvement science has several places where measurement will guide one's understanding of the implemented change and indicate if the change is working, for whom, and why. Outcome, Process, Driver, and Balance measures are the four main measures in the improvement process. These measures are embedded into the driver diagram and offer points where the scholarly practitioner can determine if their change idea is working and impacting the larger systems to achieve their broader aim. Let's take a look at each and see how they fit into the ISDiP.

Outcome measures

Outcome measures help scholarly practitioners understand the performance of the system as a whole and whether or not the change they introduce is producing an impact at the systems level. In terms of the theory of improvement, outcome measures are directly related to the aim statement and therefore should be embedded in the language of the aim statement (Bennett & Provost, 2015, p. 42). In Chapter 5, we discussed how to write an aim statement. In that statement, the scholarly practitioner should have direct items that can be measured: the goal, the timeframe for achieving the goals, and how they will determine progress. The outcomes that are in this aim statement, however, might not be immediately achievable. To accommodate that, we think of outcome measures in two ways— as leading and as lagging.

In their edX course on improvement science, the Carnegie Foundation team notes that because improvement aims are generally big and theories of improvement contain multiple drivers and change ideas that may take a long time to implement, direct impact of change ideas on the aim may take a long time. Therefore, they suggest two types of outcomes measures: lagging and leading (Carnegie Foundation, 2015.). Lagging measures speak directly to the aim statement and are lagging because it may take a long time to determine if the outcome was an improvement. Leading measures are more indicative of immediate change and can be seen in iterations of the improvement cycle that we have labeled SIAR for strategize (S), implement (I), analyze (A), and reflect (R). The SIAR cycle will be explained in Chapter 7.

For an example of this, let's return to the EdD student, Silvi, from Chapter 4 who wants to determine why the mentors in her professional physician assistant (PA) program are not effective in mentoring PA candidates. After reviewing the scholarly and professional knowledge, she develops a theory of improvement which focuses on mentor roles and student expectations as the primary drivers. She decides to pursue a change idea that focuses on these drivers. She develops training modules that teach the mentors how to better mentor and provide more useful feedback to PA candidates.

She establishes the following aim: *By January 2022, over 90% of the mentors in Lake University's PA Studies Program will be rated as "agree" or "strongly agree" on the clinical rotation evaluation questions related to the competencies of providing feedback and mentoring.* Silvi begins her ISDiP in 2019 with the goal of completing her study, defending her DiP, and graduating by 2020. For the purposes of her ISDiP, however, she will not be able to fully assess the impact of her study in this timeframe. As part of her professional practice, she plans to continue to work on her theory of improvement after graduation. Based on what she finds, she plans to do more improvement cycles with her PA candidate cohorts. In 2022, she will have data from multiple iterations of improvement cycles to determine if the training modules worked. In this case, Silvi's outcome measures to determine if the module works will be "lagging" because of her larger timeframe. In the meantime, Silvi will look at "leading" outcomes for her ISDiP, which come from several iterations of improvement cycles. As she implements each cycle, she will review the results and determine if those results indicate she is on track towards her aim. Note Figure 6.2, which offers a visual of how lagging and leading outcomes play out in Silvi's theory of improvement.

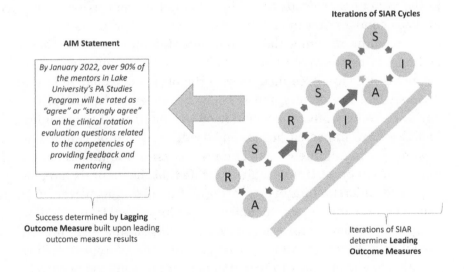

Figure 6.2. Depiction of Outcome Measures

Driver measures

Outcome measures are not enough to determine if the whole system is changing. These measures only focus on outcomes of testing changes and answer if the overall aim has been met. What happens to the rest of the system? Is it changing too? Questions like these are important. Remember that improvement science is based on systems thinking. Its purpose is not just to improve a problem, but to do so while also improving the system that produced the problem. Driver measures show if the change to the primary and secondary drivers (the *where* and the *what*) affect the system. That is, change ideas have the potential to cause observable improvement to the drivers, which then will cause change in the system at large. Whereas outcome measures let us know if the change worked (definitively), driver measures let us know if the change is working to improve the system (in progress). That is, driver measures serve as "intermediaries between the change and the outcome" (Hinnant-Crawford, 2019, p. 53).

As such, driver outcomes are closely related to the theory of improvement. They indicate if the change idea is impacting or creating observable change in the drivers, which are the key levers in the system that needs to change. If improvement is occurring in the secondary and then primary drivers, then progress is being made towards reaching the overall aim statement of the project and improving the system along the way. If the systematic change desired is not closely connected with the observable change in the drivers, then the drivers and the larger aim are misaligned. For our EdD student, Silvi, she would need to look to see if the training modules have impacted her secondary driver (mentor competencies) by examining the results of her first test of the module in an improvement cycle. If the results indicate that the mentors have an improved understanding of mentoring and are providing better feedback, then the mentor competencies have improved. If the mentor competencies have improved, her change has shifted or improved the primary driver (mentor role). As the mentor role improves, Silvi sees that she is on track to reaching her aim of students positively evaluating their mentors. Note figure 6.3 for a visual depiction of Silvi's theory of improvement and the role of driver outcomes.

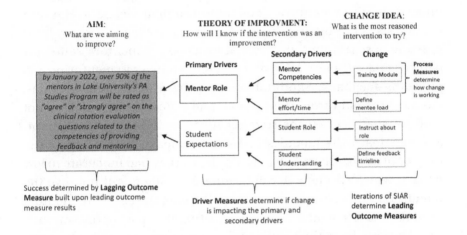

Figure 6.3. Student Example of Driver Diagram with Outcomes

Process measures

Process measures relate more directly to the improvement cycle and seek to quickly and easily answer how the change idea is working. That is, process measures tell the student if the change idea that they introduced is producing the results as they predicted. If the answer is yes, then the student should also see an impact on their driver measures and see progress towards leading outcome measures.

In determining process measures, Mintrop (2016) explains that the student must identify a unit of analysis. The unit of analysis is the subject or the entity about which the student is collecting data. The student must decide what subject or entity will best inform them about the impact of the change. Once the unit of analysis has been determined, the student then has to decide what kind of data to collect. The kind of data is directly related to the unit of analysis. Let's look at Silvi's effort to improve mentoring and feedback in her PA mentors. In her overall aim, she is trying to understand if PA candidates change their view of their mentors on the evaluations of their experience. But in the improvement cycles, she wants to understand if the training modules have changed the mentors' understanding of mentoring and improved their feedback. Her unit of analysis is the mentor. The data she will collect will come from pre- and post-training surveys that focus on the mentors' self-competence and self-perception of their competencies in mentoring and providing feedback. She implements a cycle of training modules, analyzes the data from the surveys, and reflects on whether or not (and to what degree) the training modules impacted the mentor. She may learn the modules had a high impact, in which case she might not adjust them. She may also learn they had moderate to low impact, which will help her determine how she might improve the modules. In this case, she would use the data to see where mentors need the most help and focus on adjusting that part of the training. This learning from the results of the first improvement cycle determines the process measures.

Silvi will run several more cycles to determine if the change is a true improvement and will continue to work towards her aim. As figure 6.2 indicates, other drivers and change ideas exist. Prior to her goal of 2022, she may want to implement other change ideas to reach her aim and change the system. But for the ISDiP, she will focus on this one change and do as many improvement cycles as possible in the time her EdD program allows.

Balance measures

As multiple improvement cycles happen (process outcomes) and their results impact the drivers (driver outcomes) and demonstrate that the scholarly practitioner is on track to reaching their aim (leading outcome drivers), the scholarly practitioner needs to monitor one additional measure: balance measures. Balance measures help the scholarly practitioner see if the change they have introduced has in fact been an improvement for the whole system or if it has cost the system. Process and driver outcomes from multiple improvement cycles should maintain balance in the system or improve the system

(Langley et al., 2009). If the change has disrupted the system in a negative way, then adjustments need to be made to the change idea. Again, as improvers, scholarly practitioners need to be thinking at a systems level. Therefore, balance is important. As educational leaders, they need to be aware of all aspects of their organization and how they are progressing as a result of the change. No department, area, or group of people should be adversely affected (e.g., losing staff or resources to support change in another area). The scholarly practitioner monitors balance measures along the improvement journey and continually assesses the broader impact of the change on their organization. Adjusting change ideas through the improvement cycle will help mitigate risks to unbalancing the system.

For the ISDiP, the student should report how the implementation of their change idea in improvement cycles has impacted each of these four measures. Though they will only have a short-term view, it is important that students become accustomed to thinking about these four measures as part of the improvement process. The ISDiP is often the first time students are applying improvement science in their practice. If the goal of the ISDiP is to teach them to become improvers and to have the process of improvement as a tool for addressing future problems and improving their organizations, then faculty need to be sure they are teaching improvement science from the broader systems view and preparing students to consider how to use all four measures in practice.

Gathering Data

Data for improvement is collected in the same way other data research is gathered—using qualitative, quantitative, or mixed methods. The selection of methods is determined by the change, the unit of analysis that the change is expected to impact, and the inquiry questions that the scholarly practitioner develops to guide their ability to understand if the change was an improvement. The process of designing a study and gathering data in improvement cycles is the empirical research for the ISDiP.

The design is focused on the change and how they will implement it. The scholarly practitioner develops inquiry questions to guide this process. Next, they gather data in similar ways other doctoral students do. They select the best methods for gathering the data they need, whether those be surveys, interviews, focus groups, or others, and develop qualitative or quantitative instruments or protocols. Their instruments or protocols need to be both reliable and valid, or tested to determine if questions "accurately capture the construct it is designed to capture" and results are consistent (Hinnant-Crawford, 2019, p. 51). To do this, scholarly practitioners should test their instruments with a handful of people before administering them in their improvement cycle. Doing so will determine reliability and validity of the instrument or protocol and give the scholarly practitioner a sense about how the instrument will work in their study. If at all possible, students may want to adapt established instruments or protocols for their data collection.

Different from traditional research, in improvement science, data are "collected frequently, analyzed frequently, and acted upon quickly to expedite learning about what works" (Hinnant-Crawford, 2019, p. 51). Scholarly practitioners cannot expect to be gathering data for months or years. The typical improvement cycle is 90 days (Park & Takahashi, 2013). Because the scholarly practitioner should be trying to improve their own organizations for the ISDiP, the process of gathering data quickly and frequently should be easier. The number of cycles that the student can implement during their ISDiP will determine how much they can report about achieving each of the measures. Most likely, they will report results from one to two improvement cycles. With these few cycles, they can establish process measures and may have an early determination on driver and leading outcome measures. They may also have an early indication on balance measures.

In the longer term, most scholarly practitioners will continue their improvement process after they graduate. For faculty-guiding scholarly practitioners, it is important to help the scholarly practitioner understand that the ISDiP is bounded in a shorter timeframe within a larger improvement project. Some scholarly practitioners can lose sight of this fact and may try to do too much or expect too much from the ISDiP process in terms of reaching their aim statement. Helping students see the ISDiP as a part of a larger process will also help them to understand their boundaries. It will help them to visualize the larger process as a leadership plan for their professional practice.

Designing Inquiry Courses

As a scientific research method, improvement science demands that data gathering and analysis be conducted in a disciplined and rigorous way, as it is done in traditional research. Therefore, it is important that EdD programs incorporate teaching data collection and analysis skills as part of their inquiry courses. The teaching of these skills is best done when incorporated into an improvement science course to ensure clear understanding of applying these skills to the improvement process. If data gathering and analysis methods are taught separately, for example, as part of traditional quantitative or qualitative courses, students will most likely receive broad training that will be more PhD focused, leaving scholarly practitioners to figure out how to apply data gathering and analysis methods to the improvement process. Further, as faculty backward map the design of their program, they should consider other courses where improvement science can be integrated into assignments to make it more applicable to content learning. In short, to ensure that EdD students graduate as scholarly practitioners, the program's signature methodology (in this case, improvement science) should be integrated across all course work.

Positionality

As students conduct improvement cycles in their organizations, they will be very close to the research. As practitioners, they want to see successful improvement. But as scholars, they need to remain impartial and unbiased. They are both insiders and outsiders in the research process. This is called the researcher positionality. These double roles can confuse students while they are in the research process. Further, the scholarly practitioner needs to consider their positionality in terms of their identities. In general, people have many identities and complex intersections of identities (e.g., race, professional, parental, sexuality) that shape their understanding of the world and help them make meaning (Bourke, 2014; Kezar, 2002). As part of becoming scholarly practitioners, students need to be taught to understand their researcher positionality as privileged and possess awareness about how their personal identity affects their research process in relation to their research subjects and systems of power.

To understand the researcher positionality in applied research methodologies, we turn to Herr and Anderson (2005), who identify a continuum of Insider/Outsider positions in which the scholarly practitioner is situated. Note Figure 6.4 for a description of their continuum, where we have highlighted the positions scholarly practitioners might find themselves when employing improvement science.

Insider	The scholarly practitioner is studying their own practice.
Insider collaborating with other insiders	The scholarly practitioner is studying their context in collaboration with others who are part of the organization.
Insider collaborating with outsiders	The scholarly practitioner is studying their context in collaboration with those who are outside of the organization.
Reciprocal collaboration	The scholarly practitioner works as a team with both those who are insiders and those who are outsiders.
Outsiders collaborating with insiders	The scholarly practitioner is outside of the organization studying with those who are inside.
Outsider	The scholarly practitioner is studying the organization from the outside on their own.

(adapted from Herr & Anderson, 2005)

Figure 6.4. A Description of the Insider/Outsider Continuum

Herr and Anderson (2005) explain that the "degree to which researchers position themselves as insiders or outsiders will determine how they frame epistemological, methodological, and ethical issues" (p. 39) in their DiP. For the scholarly practitioner, they must determine where they position themselves (and are systematically positioned) in their improvement journey. They must be mindful of their position as they develop their theory of improvement and design and implement their improvement cycles. They must also understand how their position influences the decisions they make throughout the improvement process. Identity positionality, then, "represents a space in which objectivism and subjectivism meet" (Bourke, 2014, p. 3).

Identity positionality asks the scholarly practitioner to consider their many identities and how they may improve or hinder the research process. Bourke (2014) explains that the "concept of self as research instrument reflects the likelihood that the researcher's own subjectivity will come to bear on the research project and any subsequent reporting of findings" (p. 2). In this sense, as the scholarly practitioner makes meaning from whether or not the change was an improvement, how they interpret results of an improvement cycle must be reconciled with the way participants make meaning of their experience with the change. How meaning is made is particularly important in improvement science, where the process is generally done with those who are part of the system and affected by the problem. In the ISDiP, scholarly practitioners should state their identities clearly. Our student, Silvi, for example, might state that she is a Hispanic, female, gay woman who has been raised in the Midwest. As she interprets the data from her improvement cycles, these identities will influence her thinking. To mitigate the degree of influence, she needs to be mindful of this fact and develop strategies to check herself and her work. Such strategies might include doing member checks, asking for participant feedback on findings, or engaging a colleague to review findings.

Pausing to consider power and privilege in improvement work

Scholarly practitioners should never approach a problem thinking that they alone have all the answers. Rushing in to "fix things" without first connecting with the individuals affected by the problem is often harmful to minoritized communities and individuals. Going in to fix a problem, even if well intended, bolsters hierarchies and power dynamics that perpetuate oppression (Bourdieu, 1973; Freire, 1970). Charity is born from inequality and has no place in improvement work (Bryk, 2017). True improvement efforts are based on mutual respect, understanding, and a willingness to listen, learn, and be useful. Those closest to the problem should have a voice. To accomplish this, it is important that scholarly practitioners become reflective and think about obstacles that could influence their work.

The first obstacle is in assuming that research is able to reveal universal truths. One of the biggest challenges to constructive improvement is in privileging one's own perspective above that of participants and community members with more marginalized voices. Even when a scholarly practitioner is part of a community (an insider), it is important to reflect on the power and privilege they hold from their identity positionality. For example, superintendents hold power over principals, White people hold more privilege than people of color, and a cisgender man may hold more power over a transgender man. Improvement work is work done in systems for systems, but it is done by individuals who inherently possess particular identities relative to those systems. Power and privilege can distort a researcher's ability to understand the problem, collect useful data, analyze measures productively, and generate useful findings. If scholarly practitioners, faculty, or mentors walk into a context without understanding their positionality, they will miss opportunities to listen and learn. To be of true service, scholarly practitioners need to understand their context deeply: the customs, beliefs, systems, and traditions that created the problem in the first place and hold it in place now. Today's educational systems and the problems embedded in them are so complex that no individual can solve them alone. Scholarly practitioners need to be a part of coordinated, collective action (Bryk, 2017). Understanding and solving problems based on the experiences of everyone is to be problem-focused and user-centered (Carnegie Foundation, 2015).

The second obstacle to productive improvement work is pride that stems from individualism. Western thinking parses individuals into weighted, binary categories that perpetuate oppressive and inaccurate stereotypes. For example, I am industrious, you are lazy; I am right, you are wrong; I am whole, you are broken; you need fixing, I can fix you. Beliefs like these create separation by "otherizing" instead of unifying. Leading with judgment instead of openness imposes dominance whether one is conscious of it or not. Advantage comes at the cost of someone else being disadvantaged. To alleviate the sense of individualism, the inequities in our schools need to be recognized and combatted. This means committing to do the work necessary to decrease achievement gaps and inequitable treatment that exist in schools and organizations for the most disadvantaged (Bourdieu, 1973; Freire, 1970; Strom & Porfilio, 2017).

The third obstacle to productive improvement is a lack of empathy and compassion. To make a difference, a scholarly practitioner needs to have an earnest desire to alleviate injustices. Empathy does not mean feeling sorry for communities, students, or families and stepping in as a savior. It means being an activist leader, tearing down the systems that foster oppression and inequity and replacing them with respect and inclusiveness (Bourdieu, 1973; Freire, 1970). To tear down these systems, one must be willing to interrogate their own beliefs, habits, and traditions. Being stuck in one's own narrative is an insidious product of privilege. Ignorance comes from fear, and fear builds the walls that fence us in as much as they fence others out. Fear inhibits the ability to think, act, and connect with empathy and compassion. If scholarly practitioners want equitable and just educational systems, or want to dismantle the systems that divide, they must begin with their own beliefs. Faculty must teach scholarly practitioners how to reconcile the injustices they see, work to create free spaces for everyone, and work collectively against oppression (Picower, 2012).

Thinking about power and privilege will also help if a review of the ISDiP design is required by the Institutional Review Board (IRB), an administrative body established to protect the rights and welfare of human subjects recruited to participate in research activities conducted under the sponsorship of an institution (Oregon State University, nd). As of 2019, new IRB regulations state that most classroom research and course assignments do not require approval. But IRB also states it is the responsibility of faculty and mentors to ensure scholarly practitioners act ethically (American University, 2019). A way to accomplish this in the ISDiP process is through self-reflection. To encourage reflection, scholarly practitioners can use questions like these:

- Do I have the professional training and competence needed to carry out the work fairly?
- Do I act with integrity?
- Am I honest, fair, and respectful of those who are different from me?
- Do I inspire trust and confidence in the individuals I work with?
- Do I respect the rights, dignity, and worth of every being?
- Am I working to eliminate bias in my own thinking and behavior?
- Am I sensitive to cultural, individual, and role differences?
- Do I acknowledge rights, values, attitudes, and opinions that differ from my own?
- Am I working to serve the individuals in my context and my profession?

Reflective questions like these should be used in any social science study (Plano Clark, & Creswell, 2010). They help scholarly practitioners identify their researcher positionality and their identity positionality and how the power and privilege that stem from these might be used for positive change.

Summary

This chapter described the four measures used in the improvement process to determine if the change has improved the problem and the system that has created the problem. The chapter also explained how these measures will be applied in the ISDiP. The chapter offered ideas for designing inquiry courses and offered perspective on the role of positionality, power, and privilege in improvement science.

Post-reading questions for faculty

1. How might the measures described above fit into your current inquiry courses? Do those courses need to be redesigned?
2. How might measures be taught as part of a leadership course on systems thinking?
3. How are you preparing scholarly practitioners to understand their positionality in their research?

Post-reading questions for scholarly practitioners/students

1. Look at your driver diagram. Can you identify where each of the four measures will fit into your theory of improvement?
2. What kinds of data will you need to collect to determine if each measure is being met? What is the unit of analysis for these?
3. Write down your positionality, both researcher and identity. How do you anticipate these might influence your improvement work? How do they influence your leadership?

References

American University (2019). Institutional Review Board: Review not Required. [Accessed 15 December 2019] Retrieved from https://www.american.edu/irb/irb-no-review.cfm

Bennett B., & Provost L, (2015). What's your theory? Driver diagram serves as tool for building and testing theories for improvement. *Quality Progress*, July. pp.36–43

Bourdieu, P. (1973). *Knowledge, education, and cultural change*. London, UK: Harper & Row Publishers.

Bourke, B. (2014). Positionality: Reflecting on the research process. *The Qualitative Report, 19*(33), 1–9.

Bryk, A. (2017). *Redressing inequities: An aspiration in search of a method.* Keynote speech presented at the Carnegie Foundation Summit on Improvement in Education, San Francisco, CA.

Carnegie Foundation. (2015). *Our ideas: Using improvement science to accelerate learning and address problems of practice.* [Accessed 18 August 2019]. Retrieved from: https://www.carnegiefoundation.org/our-ideas/

Freire, P. (1970). Pedagogy of the oppressed (MB Ramos, Trans.). *New York: Continuum*

Herr, K. & Anderson, G.L. (2005). The continuum of positionality in action research. In Herr, K., & Anderson, G.L. *The action research dissertation: A guide for students and faculty* (pp. 29–48). Thousand Oaks, CA: SAGE Publications, Inc. https://dx.doi.org/10.4135/9781452226644.n3

Hinnant-Crawford, B.N. (2019). Practical measurement in improvement science. In Crow, R., Hinnant-Crawford, B.N, & Spaulding, D.T. (Eds). *The educational leader's guide to improvement science: Data, design, and cases for reflection.* Myers Education Press: Gorham, ME.

Kezar, A. (2002). Reconstructing Static Images of Leadership: An Application of Positionality Theory. *Journal of Leadership Studies, 8*(3), 94–109. https://doi.org/10.1177/107179190200800308

Langley, G., Moen, R., Nolan, K., Nolan, T., Norman, C., & Provost, L. (2009). *The improvement guide: A practical approach to enhancing organizational performance* (2nd ed.). San Francisco, CA: Jossey-Bass.

LeMahieu, P., Edwards, A., & Gomez, L. (2015). At the nexus of improvement science and teaching: Introduction to a special section of the Journal of Teacher Education. *Journal of Teacher Education, 66*(5), 446–449.

MichiganX. (Producer). LeadEd503x: Improvement science in education [Video]. Retrieved from https://courses.edx.org/courses/course-1:MichiganX+LeadEd503x+2T2019/course/

Mintrop, R. (2016). *Design-based school improvement: A practical guide for education leaders.* Cambridge, MA: Harvard Education Press.

Oregon State University, (nd). What is the Institutional Review Board (IRB)? Downloaded from https://research.oregonstate.edu/irb/frequently-asked-questions/what-institutional-review-board-irb

Park, S. & Takahashi, S. (2013). 90-day cycle handbook. Palo Alto, CA: Carnegie Foundation for the Advancement of Teaching.

Picower, B. (2012). Teacher activism: Enacting a vision for social justice. *Equity & Excellence in Education, 45*(4), 561–574.

Plano Clark, V.L., & Creswell, J.W. (2010). *Understanding research: A consumer's guide.* Boston, MA: Pearson.

Solberg, L.I., Mosser, G., & McDonald, S. (1997). The three faces of performance measurement: Improvement, accountability, and research. The Joint Commission *Journal on Quality Improvement, 23*(3), pp. 135–147.

Strom, K., & Porfilio, B. (2017). Centering social justice in EdD programs. *Impacting Education, 2*(1), 15–19.

CHAPTER SEVEN

Testing the Theory/Change and Final Write Up

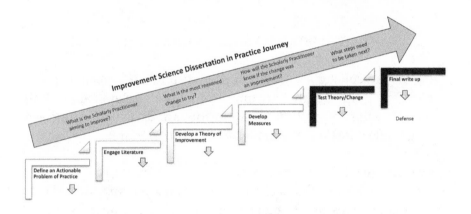

Figure 7.1. Improvement Science Dissertation in Practice (ISDiP) Journey Test Change/Theory and Final Write Up

> Improvement begins in our will, but to achieve improvement we need a method for systemic change, a model for improvement. (Berwick, 1996, p. 620)

The previous chapters have explained why improvement science is a reasoned structure for a dissertation in practice and offered steps to get started: how to find an actionable, high-leverage problem of practice (PoP), how to use literature to understand how others have approached the problem, how to develop an aim and theory of improvement, and how to develop measures to understand if the posed change truly is an improvement. This chapter explains the next steps in the ISDiP process: implementing the change effort. For many scholarly practitioners, this phase of the improvement journey is the most exciting part because it is the time when they get to take action and see the efforts of their hard work. In this chapter we explain our Model of Improvement, pause to reflect on power and privilege in improvement work, explain how cycles of improvement fit into an EdD program and into an ISDiP, and provide ideas for quality standards for this work.

The ISDiP Model of Improvement

Langley and colleagues (2009) devised a simple yet elegant model for achieving changes that are improvements. Langley et al.'s (2009) model is comprised of three basic questions and a cycle for testing a change. The questions the model seeks to answer are:

- What are we trying to accomplish?
- How will I know that a change is an improvement?
- What changes can we make that will result in improvement?

Underneath these questions lies a plan-do-study-act (PDSA) cycle, which is a framework used to answer the three improvement questions. Planning (P) consists of asking questions, designing a change, making predictions about the change, and designing measures to determine if the change made a difference. Doing (D) consists of carrying out the change effort and collecting data on it, paying special attention to implementation challenges and unexpected consequences. Studying (S) is analyzing the data, comparing it to predictions, and summarizing. Acting (A) consists of making decisions about the change (should it be adjusted, expanded, or abandoned?) and formulating the next steps (Langely, et al., 2009). Figure 7.2 demonstrates our model, which is built upon Langley et al. (2009). Our model is different in that it has been tailored to the dissertation in practice (DiP).

ISDiP Model of Improvement

Fundamental questions to guide the improvement effort

What is the Scholarly Practitioner aiming to improve?	What is the most reasoned change to try?
How will the Scholarly Practitioner know if the change was an improvement?	What steps need to be taken next?

Framework for trial and effort methodology

Strategize

Reflect — Inquiry questions — Implement

Analyze

Figure 7.2. ISDiP Model of Improvement

Like the Langley et al. (2009) model, our model has fundamental questions on the top that guide the improvement effort and a framework at the bottom that is circular and iterative. However, unlike

Langley et al.'s model, ours is designed to develop the leadership and intellectual skills EdD scholarly practitioners need to lead improvement efforts in their educational organizations. Our model is tied to the DiP, which we see as a process of formation (Elkana, 2006; Walker, Golde, Jones, Bueschel, & Hutchings, 2008). Through coursework and dissertation study, scholarly practitioners develop a professional identity as improvers, critical thinkers, and adaptive, reflective, translational leaders.

Questions on our model

The improvement questions on our ISDiP model are similar in purpose to those in the Model of Improvement (Langley et al., 2009) but they differ in context and reason. Like Langley et al.'s (2009), our model's questions focus on problems embedded in practice. However, our model has questions aimed at developing scholarly practitioners' ability to find actionable problems within their own contexts, blend their professional knowledge with literature to develop and implement a reasoned change, measure the change, and then decide what to do next. The ISDiP Model of Improvement asks:

- What is the scholarly practitioner aiming to improve?
- What is the most reasoned change to try?
- How will the scholarly practitioner know if the change was an improvement?
- What steps need to be taken next?

These questions guide change efforts, cycles of work on them, and, as Figure 2.1 shows, the dissertation journey. Our model's questions are designed to develop scholarly practitioners who have the knowledge, skills, and dispositions of an improver.

PDSA cycles versus SIAR cycles

In Langely et al.'s (2009) Model of Improvement, the PDSA cycles turn ideas into action and connect that action to learning. Our model does the same, but rather than use the words plan, do, study, and act, we use words aimed at critical thinking and leadership capabilities. In the SIAR, cycle improvers strategize (S), implement (I), analyze (A), and reflect (R) on the changes they make and efforts they lead (each of these is explained more below). See Table 7.1, which compares definitions in a typical school improvement PDSA and a SIAR in a doctoral program.

Table 7.1. Comparing PDSA to SIAR

PDSA	SIAR
Plan To think about and arrange the parts or details of (something) before it happens (Merriam-Webster, n.d.). Planning for improvement, according to Milder & Lorr (2018), entails: • defining the change; • making predictions about it; and • designing a way to test the change on an appropriate scale.	Strategize To devise a course of action: to make a plan for achieving a goal (Merriam-Webster, n.d.). Strategizing for improvement entails: • working collaboratively on an implementation plan; • being proactive to anticipate problems; • leading purposefully and creatively; • turning to literature and experts to gain insight; • remaining realistically optimistic; • collaborating with those who have differing viewpoints; and working non-judgmentally.
Do To perform (an action or activity) (Merriam-Webster, n.d.). Doing, according to Milder & Lorr (2018), entails: • carrying out the change; • collecting data; and • documenting how implementation went.	Implement To begin to do or use (something, such as a plan): to make (something) active or effective (Merriam-Webster, n.d.). Implementing for improvement entails: • inspiring others to work to answer the inquiry questions; • engaging resisters; • getting the right people working on the right tasks; • being adaptive, understanding improvement is not linear; • prioritizing tasks; • taking reasoned risks; • observing, listening, and documenting without bias; and • working fairly, ethically, along-side, and as hard as others.

PDSA	**SIAR**
Study	Analyze
An organized experiment in which many things are looked at, measured, recorded, etc., in order to learn more about something (Merriam-Webster, n.d.). Studying for improvement, according to Milder & Lorr (2018), entails: • analyzing the data; • comparing findings to predictions; and • gleaning insights.	To study (something) closely and carefully: to learn the nature and relationship of the parts of (something) by a close and careful examination (Merriam-Webster, n.d.). Analyzing for improvement entails: • collecting and analyzing data fairly and ethically—striving to understand what worked, for who, and why and who is left off; • looking for, and recognizing, patterns; • suspending judgment—interpreting data objectively, fairly, and without bias; • drawing conclusions with caution; • asking thoughtful questions about findings; • identifying various conclusions that are possible and deciding which (if any) are sufficiently supported; • weighing strengths and limitations of all options; and • not rushing to conclusions or making hasty judgments.
Act	Reflect
To do something: to take action (Merriam-Webster, n.d.). Acting, according to Milder & Lorr (2018), entails using what was learned to decide what to do next.	To think carefully about something: to think or say (something) after careful thought (Merriam-Webster, 2019, n.d.). Reflecting on improvement entails: • stepping back—looking at what occurred through others' eyes; • being aware of the many and varied ways knowledge is displayed; • being self-aware—looking back on one's actions, choices, and decisions; • resisting unfair assumptions, thoughtlessness, conformity, fear of change, bias, and egocentric conclusions; • continually asking why; and strategizing what's next.

SIAR template

While working on their ISDiP, it is likely that scholarly practitioners will need to do several trial SIAR cycles. Mini-SIAR cycles can be used to understand the initial reactions to better understand the problem, gain insight into the change idea, and refine products or processes. Mini-cycles support, enrich, and help ensure smooth implementation of the final 90-day SIAR. The final cycle occurs later in a program after much exploration and groundwork have been completed. That is, by the time the SIAR is ready to be implemented, the scholarly practitioner will have:

- investigated the practitioner context;
- selected an actionable PoP and unpacked it with a fishbone;
- performed a Review of Scholarly and Professional Knowledge to understand the problem and how others have approached it;
- collaboratively developed an aim and theory of improvement;
- performed some small, investigative SIAR cycles;
- used all of the above to develop inquiry questions;
- created a change idea;
- developed methods and measures to understand if the change will be an improvement; and
- secured permissions (e.g., Institutional Review Board, district consent, participant agreements).

This groundwork is completed throughout the EdD program and lays the foundation for the 90-day SIAR, which occurs near the end of the program. The 90-day SIAR has key parts and, because of this, we have developed a template to guide scholarly practitioners. Note Figure 7.3. We explain each step next.

Strategize

The success of any strategy depends on the goal and how realistic, detailed, and organized the plan is to achieve it. Given this, strategizing is the first step in the 90-day SIAR cycle (see upper left corner in Figure 7.3). To strategize, the scholarly practitioner should carefully work out each detail before implementation. The following questions can guide the strategizing phase: Who will comprise the research team? What will each person be expected to do (e.g., implement the

SIAR Template

| Change idea implemented: | | | | Tester: | |
| Goal: | | | | Date: | |

Strategize			**Analyze**
Inquiry Questions	Predictions/Hypothesis	Methods/Measures	Results
Q 1			
Q 2			
Q 3			
Q 4			
Team:			Was the intervention successful? What did you learn?
Details: who/what/where/when/how and how long			
Resources:			
Norms:			

Implement	**Reflect**
Objectively describe what happened. Did implementation go as planned? Were there any obstacles/surprises in implementation or any difficulty with measures?	On the intervention
Document the results. Comment on the inquiry questions and predictions. Were they correct? Record any data summaries as well.	On self as leader

Figure 7.3. SIAR Template

change, collect/analyze data)? What resources need to be gathered? What norms of engagement will be used? Strategizing for each SIAR cycle will vary, so modification will be necessary. When strategizing, the scholarly practitioner should do so with an equity lens. Here are questions to ask to strategize for equity:

- How is the implementation plan designed to interrupt inequitable practices?
- When strategizing the implementation plan, whose voices are needed? Are there any omitted?
- How was a strength-based as opposed to a deficit-based frame used in designing the plan?
- Does the plan connect with the lived experience of those affected by the problem?
- How is local wisdom integrated into the plan?
- Are the necessary resources fairly distributed?
- Are the predictions/hypothesis fair?

Implement

The implementation phase of the ISDiP is when the action happens, and it tends to be the most exciting for scholarly practitioners. Implementation in the SIAR means getting the change effort going, thoroughly and objectively describing what is happening, collecting evidence to understand what is working, for whom, and why, and documenting how things went overall (see bottom left of Figure 7.3). Equity should be part of the implementation plan as well. Here are questions to ask to implement for equity:

- Are those closest to the problem part of the implementation team?
- What has been done to ensure data collection is equitable and just?
- How will issues of power bias be addressed during implementation?
- How will differing values, attitudes, and opinions be gathered?
- How will all voices be heard?

Analyze

After the change has been implemented and data have been collected, the data needs to be analyzed, displayed, and interpreted. This process allows the scholarly practitioners to determine if the change worked and to learn from what happened (see top right of Figure 7.3). Analysis, like in the other phases, should also have an equity lens. Here are some questions to ask to analyze for equity:

- How will analysis lead to an understanding of the systemic inequities that exist?
- Does the analysis team have members with varied perspectives?
- Are those affected by the problem part of the team?
- How will progress toward the aim be determined?
- What norms will the analysis team use?
- How will bias be eliminated from analysis?
- How will results be displayed so everyone affected by the problem can understand the results?

- Were all voices heard?
- How will diverse groups gain access to the findings?

Reflect

This final phase the SIAR cycle (bottom right of Figure 7.3) is the time to reflect on oneself as a leader and reflect on the change process. When scholarly practitioners reflect on themselves as leaders, they should look back on themselves as leaders involved in an improvement process and document how they handled this role by understanding what successes and struggles they had and how they responded. When scholarly practitioners reflect, they should also explain how the work contributes to their personal and professional goals, how they envision the continued use of improvement science in their practice, and how their findings contribute to professional knowledge. This phase of the SIAR is a personal experience and should focus on oneself as an equitable leader. Here are some questions to ask to reflect for equity:

- Did the improvement process make things better for marginalized voices?
- How will the next cycle be designed for more diversity and inclusion?
- How will spreading, scaling up, or sustaining make things more equitable and just?
- How will new and diverse individuals be brought into the process?

Next, reflecting on the change process requires thinking about the next steps for improving. Educators and organizational leaders understand that problems of practice are complex and know their work will never be complete. Even with successful changes, most scholarly practitioners remain curious to find ways to enlarge, spread, or sustain the improvements they make.

"Enlarging" refers to deliberately scaling up the effort started in the ISDiP. Ramping up is performed by:

a) testing the change with more participants;
b) testing the change in new and different contexts;
c) testing the change again within its current context; and
d) testing the change in other areas/disciplines (New York City Department of Education, 2018).

Scholarly practitioners should consider enlarging as an opportunity to expand their sphere of influence and contribute to the profession.

"Spreading" refers to the process of moving the change effort across more settings (e.g., from one classroom to district-wide, from organization A to organizations, B, C, and D). Spreading is important. However, a scholarly practitioner must realize that spreading change presents new and different challenges. When a change is spread, it is important to:

a) simplify the change for its new contexts;
b) consider the number individuals involved. The spread of a change should never outpace the capacities of the individuals implementing it. When spreading ideas, be sure to include time and support; and
c) use narratives. Stories and testimonials are the quickest and most memorable way to share successful changes. Collecting the stories from those affected is a powerful way to spread ideas (New York City Department of Education, 2018).

"Sustaining" refers to keeping the momentum of the change after the scholarly practitioner has left the context. Sustaining means finding and training individuals who can carry on the work. Adler and Karlsberg (n.d.) suggest steps for sustaining an innovation that scholarly practitioners should consider. These include:

• establishing a new aim and sense of direction;
• developing new inquiry questions;
• opening communication channels;
• instilling a sense of ownership; and
• ensuring there will be rewards and recognition for those carrying out the work.

Performing SIAR cycles in the DiP provides scholarly practitioners the skills they need to address high-leverage problems that matter to them and their contexts. Additionally, this process provides opportunity for scholarly practitioners to display leadership capabilities and attempt to close the chasm between practice and scholarship for the most disadvantaged students and communities (Bryk, 2017; Bryk, et al., 2011).

How ISDiPs Fit in EdD Programs

> The goal of the PhD is to understand the world. The goal of the EdD is to change the world. (Kirk as cited in Wergin, 2011, p 19)

The quote above nicely captures the distinction between the EdD and PhD and helps us understand that each degree needs to be distinctive. EdD programs should prepare their students to change the world through the transformation of practice just as PhD programs should prepare their students to study the world and, in turn, transform the knowledge of a discipline (Council of Graduate Schools, 2007). While total consensus on what this looks like is currently lacking, a number of commonalities are emerging around each degree's objective, knowledge base, research, and dissertation (Young, 2006). Note Table 7.2.

Table 7.2 shows that EdD graduates should be prepared differently than PhD graduates. EdD programs should help their students become reflective, professional leaders that are competent in identifying and solving problems of practice. To accomplish this, EdD programs should enrich their students' wealth of professional experience with research and practical theory. EdD programs should prepare students to design and lead changes and be able to measure the effect of what they do. Their dissertation should be aimed at decision-oriented problem solving, skills that will transfer into their professional life (Young, 2006). DiPs should allow students to continue working while they complete their degree and to obtain their degree in a reasonable amount of time, typically no more than three

Table 7.2. EdD Programs vs. PhD Programs

EdD	PhD
Degree Objective	Degree Objective
Preparation of professional leaders competent in identifying and solving complex problems in education. Emphasis is on developing thoughtful and reflective practitioners.	Preparation of professional researchers, scholars, or scholarly practitioners. Develops competence in conducting scholarship and research that focuses on acquiring new knowledge.
Knowledge Base	Knowledge Base
Develops and applies knowledge for practice. Research-based content themes and theory are integrated with practice with emphasis on application of knowledge base.	Fosters theoretical and conceptual knowledge. Content is investigative in nature with an emphasis on understanding the relationships to leadership practice and policy.
Research Methods	Research Methods
Develops an overview and understanding of research including data collection skills for action research, program measurement, and program evaluation. Could include work in management statistics and analysis.	Courses are comparable to doctoral courses in related disciplines. Courses develop an understanding of inquiry and qualitative and quantitative research. Developing competencies in research design, analysis, synthesis, and writing.
Dissertation	Dissertation
Well-designed applied research of value for informing educational practice. Reflects theory or knowledge for addressing decision-oriented problems in applied settings.	Original research illustrating a mastery of competing theories with the clear goal of informing disciplinary knowledge (Young, 2006).

years. This timeframe is challenging because it requires much be accomplished in a short amount of time. To keep up, scholarly practitioners must take two to three courses per semester, including the summer, and they must work on their DiPs along the way. Given these parameters, DiP work should start early, in the first class, and build throughout each component of the program. What this might look like in a 3-year EdD program is noted in Figure 7.4. Figure 7.4 may also be thought of as sections/chapters of an ISDiP and we elaborate on this idea next.

ISDiP in a Program of Study

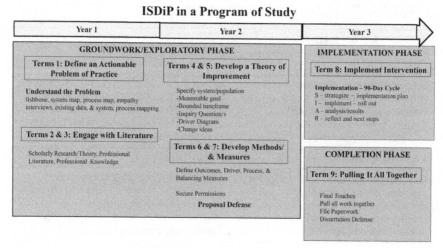

Figure 7.4. ISDiP Program Map

Groundwork/exploratory phase

Term one: Define an actionable problem of practice

During term one, scholarly practitioners begin observing their context and working with others to define an actionable problem of practice. During this process, tools like a fishbone diagram, system map, process map, empathy interviews, and existing data should be employed to understand the nature, roots, and severity of their problem as it exists in their local context.

Terms two and three: Engage with literature

During terms two and three, scholarly practitioners are taught to find and review scholarly and professional literature in order to understand what others have discovered about their problem. Their learning is applied to their review of scholarly and professional knowledge and supports the development of a conceptual framework that situates their problem. Engaging the literature continues throughout the ISDiP to inform the theory of improvement and the data analysis. Further, it becomes a habit and part of their professional practice.

Terms four and five: Develop a theory of improvement

During terms four and five, the literature, the fishbone, and other information gathered are used to create a driver diagram, a visual depiction that contains an aim statement, primary and secondary systems drivers, and change ideas. The driver diagram is the scholarly practitioner's working theory of improvement that guides the development of their inquiry questions and change ideas that will be tested during the SIAR.

Terms six and seven: Develop methods and measures

During terms six and seven, scholarly practitioners develop their methodology/measurement plan. This plan should contain the process that will be used to collect data, the measures (driver, process, and balancing) that will be used, and the analysis plan. Because scholarly practitioners have been working on their dissertation over the past semesters, they should now be ready to secure permissions and obtain IRB approval. Near the mid to end of term seven, scholarly practitioners should defend an overview of their DiP plan and move on to implementation of their change idea. Note that several mini-SIAR cycles should be performed during these and earlier terms to gain insight into the change idea prior to the 90-day cycle.

Implementation phase

Term eight: Implement the change

During term eight, scholarly practitioners implement the change. Term eight contains a 90-day SIAR cycle, where scholarly practitioners strategize an implementation plan (S), implement it (I), measure and analyze what occurred (A), and decide on the next steps (Reflect). This 90-day structure is the place where the inquiry questions are investigated, data is gathered and analyzed, and conclusions are drawn. Doing a 90-day cycle is intentional in improvement work. The goal is to learn quickly and adjust to attain improvement. The cycle also keeps scholarly practitioners on track towards graduation.

Final Work and Defense Phase

Term nine: Finalizing

The final term gives scholarly practitioners time to pull their work together into a presentation for both their faculty and their organizations. This product might come in an academic format, a practitioner format, or both. It might also take an alternative format, such as a digital form or presentation. The design depends on the institution and its policies. During this time, students also file necessary paperwork for their defense and graduation.

We realize that this progression may not be for every scholarly practitioner or program because contexts, cultures, affordances, and constraints vary. Some programs have semesters while others have terms or quarters. Think of Figure 7.2 as a flexible template faculty and scholarly practitioners can adopt or adapt to fit to institutional needs.

Thoughts on the Final Write Up: ISDiP Parts and Quality

The final term gives scholarly practitioners time to pull their work together into a presentation for both their faculty and their organizations. Products likely vary from academic format, a practitioner format, or both. No matter what the form, the scholarly practitioner should be concerned with completeness and quality in content, thinking, and presentation. To assist scholarly practitioners in achieving this, we have developed a template in Table 7.3. However, this template is not meant to be prescriptive or static. We encourage scholarly practitioners, faculty, and committee members to adapt it to fit their own dissertations and needs.

Table 7.3. ISDiP Parts

Title and Abstract	
Title	Succinctly captures the actionable problem of practice and change idea.
Abstract	Is structured and contains: an actionable PoP, who will be involved in, and affected by, the change, how the change will be measured, findings, conclusions, and next steps.
Groundwork/Exploratory	
Defines the Actionable PoP	Describes the problem from the perspective of those who are nearest to it (what was learned from the fishbone, system map, empathy interviews, existing data, etc.).
	Describes the context and scholarly practitioner's responsibility, authority and intimate knowledge of the problem.
	Captures the significance of the PoP for practice.
Reviews Scholarly & Professional Knowledge	Summarizes what is currently known about the problem, its potential solution, and ways to measure it.
	Includes information from relevant studies, practical articles, professional knowledge, expert knowledge, etc.
Implementation—90-Day Cycle	
Explains the Theory of Improvement/Change	Specifies the system/population.
	Provides and explains what was found from the driver diagram (aim, drivers, and change ideas).
	States the inquiry question(s).
	Explains the change idea, its implementation plan, and bounded timeframe.
Documents Measures	Explains the measures (process, driver, balancing, or outcome) used to study the change (who they were used with, when, how, and why).
	Justifies the use of each measure (validity/reliability, credibility, and trustworthiness).
Provides Analysis of measures	Documents the analysis plan—includes sense-making strategies and ways analysis was fair and unbiased.
Ethical Considerations	Includes (in an appendix) permissions secured.

Results	
Results	Explains what occurred as a result of the change—includes convergence and consonance as well as divergence and dissonance of measures.
	Displays findings visually (tables, graphs, etc.).
Discussion	
Discussion	Discusses key finding relevant to the impact of the change on the PoP, individuals, policies, materials, products and/or practices.
	Explains the strengths and weaknesses of the change and overall process.
Provides Next Steps	Explains ideas to enlarge, spread, and/or sustain the work.
Final Reflection	Captures what the scholarly practitioner learned as a collaborative leader involved in an improvement process.
Lessons Learned	Documents lessons learned for practice, education, and/or policy

Summary

This chapter explained the ISDiP Model of Improvement as a means for scholarly practitioners to test their change ideas. The chapter explained the model's four improvement questions and SIAR cycle and how they apply to the DiP. It also paused to encourage faculty, mentors, and scholarly practitioners to think about their power and privilege as they perform improvement work. An example of how a 90-day SIAR cycle could fit into a three-year EdD program and how SIARs fit into an ISDiP were offered, along with a template to ensure coverage and quality.

Post-reading questions for faculty

1. Our Model of Improvement is different from others. Can you think of ways you might alter our model to fit the needs of the scholarly practitioners you work with?
2. We have provided a possible plan of study for an EdD student

doing an ISDiP. In your context, what changes would need to be made to allow completion in 3 years?

3. We propose scholarly practitioners do their ISDiP 90-day SIAR at the beginning of their third year. What would need to be done for this idea to fit into your EdD program?

4. We have provided ideas for a quality ISDiP. What does this capture correctly? What is missing from it?

Post-reading questions for scholarly practitioners/students

1. Our Model of Improvement is different from others. How do you think it captures your needs?

2. We have provided a possible plan of study for an EdD student doing an ISDiP. What would the benefits and drawbacks of this plan be for you?

3. We have provided ideas for a quality ISDiP. What does this table capture correctly? What is missing from it for you?

References

Adler, J., & Karlsberg, R. (n.d.). 7 strategies for sustained innovation. *InnovationManagement*. Retrieved 8 December 2019, from https://innovationmanagement.se/imtool-articles/7-strategies-for-sustained-innovation/

Berwick, D.M. (1996). A primer on leading the improvement of systems. *BMJ, 312*(7031), 619–622.

Bryk, A. (2017). *Redressing inequities: An aspiration in search of a method.* Carnegie Foundation for the Advancement of Teaching Keynote speech presented at the Carnegie Foundation Summit on Improvement in Education, San Francisco, CA.

Bryk, A.S., Gomez, L.M., Gunrow, A., & LeMahieu, P.G. (2017). *Learning to improve: How America's schools can get better at getting better.* Cambridge, MA, Harvard Education Press.

Bryk, A.S, Gomez, L.M., & Grunow, A., (2011). *Getting ideas into action: Building networked improvement communities in education.* Carnegie

Foundation for the Advancement of Teaching. Retrieved 4 September, 2019, from https://www.carnegiefoundation.org/resources/publications/getting-ideas-action-building-networked-improvement-communities-education/

Carnegie Foundation. (n.d.). *Our ideas.* Retrieved 8 December 2019, from: https://www.carnegiefoundation.org/our-ideas/

Council of Graduate Schools (2007). *Task force report on the professional doctorate.* Washington, DC.

Elkana, Y. (2006). Unmasking uncertainties and embracing contradictions: Graduate education in the sciences. In C.M. Golde and G.E. Walker (eds.), *Envisioning the future of doctoral education: Preparing stewards of the discipline, Carnegie essays on the doctorate*, pp. 65–96. San Francisco: Jossey-Bass.

Langley G.L., Moen R., Nolan K.M., Nolan, T.W., Norman, C.L., & Provost, L.P. (2009). *The improvement guide: A practical approach to enhancing organizational performance* (2nd edition). San Francisco: Jossey-Bass.

Merriam-Webster Dictionary (n.d.). Retrieved 5 January, 2020 from, https://www.merriam-webster.com/dictionary/

New York City Department of Education. (2018). *Improvement science handbook: Empowering New York educators to make progress on critical issues that stand in the way of student success.* Retrieved 29 November 2019 from, https://www.weteachnyc.org/media2016/filer_public/4b/40/4b4027b3-c0a6-4129-a050-7c41120a38d7/nycdoe_improvement_science_handbook_2018_online.pdf

Picower, B. (2012). Teacher activism: Enacting a vision for social justice. *Equity & Excellence in Education, 45*(4), 561–574.

Plano Clark, V.L., & Creswell, J.W. (2010). Understanding research: A consumer's guide. Pearson, Boston, MA.

Strom, K., & Porfilio, B. (2017). Centering social justice in EdD programs. *Impacting Education, 2*(1), 15–19.

Walker, G.E., Golde, C.M., Jones, L., Bueschel, A.C., & Hutchings, P. (2008). *The formation of scholars: Rethinking doctoral education for the twenty-first century.* San Francisco: Jossey-Bass.

Wergin, J.F. (2011). Rebooting the EdD. *Harvard Educational Review 81*(1), 119–139.

Young, M.D. (2006). The M.Ed., Ed. D., and Ph. D. in educational leadership. *UCEA Review, 48*(2), 6–9.

CHAPTER EIGHT

Implications:

Challenges and Lessons Learned

The chapters in this book have provided an overview of the EdD as *the* degree for working professionals, a reason why an improvement science dissertation in practice (ISDiP) fits the needs of these professionals, and a demonstration of how to use the tools and processes of improvement science as a dissertation frame. This chapter continues the conversation with the challenges and lessons we have learned working with faculty, committee members, and scholarly practitioners while implementing improvement science in dissertations in practice (DiPs). The chapter begins with challenges and ideas for faculty and committee members. Then, it moves on to similar ideas for scholarly practitioners.

Challenges for Faculty and Committee Members

Change in higher education comes slowly because of its strong culture and entrenched traditions, like the dissertation (Kennedy, et al., 2018; Perry, 2014; Schuster & Finkelstein, 2006; Tierney, 1998). Pioneers of change do, however, exist. For example, in 2014, Nick Sousanis, an EdD student at Columbia University's Teachers College, was given permission to write and draw his dissertation in comic book form. Sousanis's (2014) dissertation, *Unflattening: A Visual-Verbal Inquiry Into Learning in Many Dimensions*, broke traditional norms by weaving together philosophical essays and theory with graphic images. His work made a profound contribution to the study of comics, semiotics, epistemology, and visual thinking. The work also impacted practice by becoming recommended reading for students wanting to utilize visual narrative form (Dunn, 2014). Yet, despite this innovation, Sousanis's work posed challenges alongside those rewards for thinking about dissertation redesign.

Sousanis did not choose the comic book medium because he felt it would be easy. He chose it, rather, because he is a visual learner, and as a teacher, he had success using it with his own students. Sousanis had an intuitive notion and wanted to investigate the usefulness of visuals on learning. He wanted to work hard to build an intellectual argument that would not only stand up to academic scrutiny but also be meaningful for other visual learners as a visual representation of his intellectual premise. Sousanis's dissertation has been successful on each of these fronts. He was granted an EdD and in 2015, Harvard University Press published his dissertation in a book called *Unflattening*. Sousanis is a prime example of a doctoral student who thought outside the narrow confines of dissertation guidelines and used this exercise to impact practice. His success should be a wake-up call for other students and faculty members to stretch boundaries. To Sousanis, dissertations should not be a one-size-fits-all product (Dunn, 2014).

Sousanis was successful because he worked hard and was mentored well. Dr. Ruth Vinz, Sousanis's main adviser, had her own perspectives of dissertations. She believed dissertations should be more than just an institutional requirement, or hoop to jump through (Dunn, 2014). Vinz believed that a dissertation should capture a student's knowledge, show how they make meaning, and provide a way for that student to share their findings with others. As she worked with Sousanis, Vinz quickly realized that he created meaning visually as well as verbally, so she was bold enough to afford him that freedom. Vinz told Sousanis to take risks, trust his talents, and not let form get in the way of substance (Dunn, 2014). She was right.

Sousanis's dissertation work has encouraged other doctoral students to advocate for arts-based dissertations. Because of EdD students like Sousanis and other PhD students, there has been a push for new types and forms of dissertations. Task forces have been formed, and reports, books, and articles have been written about the dissertation dilemma. Some working on this pose possible solutions, like casting the dissertation into the dustbin of history, whereas others want to redesign it for twenty-first century needs (Patton, 2013).

Despite varied opinions about the purpose and format of dissertations, there is no indication that they will be removed from education doctoral preparation any time soon. Colleges and universities can be very traditional institutions, and faculty resist change in an effort to maintain the status quo. However, there are innovators, like Sousanis and Dr. Ruth Vinz, individuals with a vision who are willing to work hard to change the status quo.

Like Sousanis, EdD students should have the opportunity to make their dissertations useful to them and their contexts. Their scholarship should solve educational problems and disrupt what is known about the location of knowledge (Gutierrez & Penuel, 2014; Ravitch & Lytle, 2016). Faculty working in EdD programs who only use their PhD experience and require dissertations like their own miss the opportunity to help practitioners cross the theory to practice divide. Practitioners are asking questions about research like: *Why was this study designed and who designed it? How did practice inform this work? What are the unintended consequences?* and, most importantly, *Who benefitted?* (Erickson & Gutiérrez, 2002; Gutiérrez & Penuel, 2014; Gutiérrez & Vossoughi, 2010). Questions like these can be answered if improvement science is used as an inquiry frame because it:

- addresses specific problems and answers the questions practicing educators need answers to;
- is anchored in experiences of people actually engaged in the work;
- integrates what those closest to the problem know with extant research-based knowledge; and

- sees educators as active inquirers bound together with values and norms akin to a scientific community (Bryk et al., 2015).

Given these, shaping dissertations around improvement science may begin to lessen the skepticism between research and practice. Faculty in EdD programs need to question the usefulness of an entrenched tradition, like the dissertation, for their students. The next section offers ideas to get started.

Lessons learned

Changing dissertations is difficult and complex work, but faculty associated with CPED-influenced programs are working to make this culminating experience more useful for the working professionals in their programs. One way to make programmatic changes based on CPED's Framework was explained in Chapter 1 with the idea of backward mapping: starting with graduate outcomes (the end) and one-by-one, changing program components to achieve desired outcomes (Thomson, et al., 2017).

Here, we expand on these ideas and offer four lessons to support the redesign of dissertations using improvement science. Our lessons come from our experiences redesigning our own programs, working with others in redesigning theirs, writing manuscripts on redesign efforts, and attending CPED convenings and other academic meetings. Our four lessons focus on admissions, pedagogy, courses, and mentoring.

Start with admissions

Ensuring EdD programs prepare graduates with the outcomes they need begins with selecting students who fit the program. Faculty need to ensure students come with the foundation necessary to be successful. To that end, we recommend the following tips to determine the best candidates for EdD programs:

- Have applicants describe a problem of practice (PoP) they seek to improve through their dissertation experience. Even though their problems may not be fully articulated, the type of problem posed can determine fit with your program. Is the problem practical, a true PoP, or is it theoretical, one that would be better answered by a student in a PhD program?

- Confirm that applicants have a professional setting, which can serve as a laboratory of practice or as a cooperative context in which they can apply what they learn and conduct their dissertation work. The aim of an ISDiP is to have students change their organizations. Therefore, they need to be in a professional position as they enter the program.

- Ask applicants to state their professional goals associated with receiving a doctorate. If they write about teaching in a university or continuing to research, they most likely are a better fit for a PhD program. If they want to remain in their professional position or advance in practice, the EdD is the best fit.

Teach improvement science at a doctoral level

Improvement science should not be taught as a module or a short workshop. Rather, it needs to be an integral part of the program or the core inquiry courses. Students need persistent and consistent practice, utilizing the tools and understanding the underlying theory of improvement science. To that end, programs should:

- use a signature pedagogy to teach improvement science deliberately and pervasively;
- teach the deep meaning of improvement work;
- ensure scholarly practitioners understand its traditions, use in other professions, and why and how improvement science is scientific (see Chapter 2);
- teach scholarly practitioners to use and analyze the tools of improvement without bias or assumptions;
- require students to think critically about their assumptions, power, and privilege;
- teach scholarly practitioners to decode, decipher, and apply literature to clarify PoPs, develop interventions, and gain insight into practical measures;

- teach scholarly practitioners how to develop valid measurement tools;
- teach the data gathering and analysis tools of quantitative, qualitative, and mixed methods in applied ways to help students understand when, how, and why to use each to measure improvement efforts (e.g., a survey as a balancing measure, a test as an outcome measure, an interview as a driver measure); and
- teach visual and other innovative ways to display results.

Ensure courses align and support students doing ISDiPs

Backward mapping a program means working back from the graduate competencies identified by the program through each programmatic component starting with the dissertation. To ensure students are prepared to do an ISDiP, inquiry courses, foundation courses, and specialization courses all must align towards the ISDiP. To that end, programs must:

- have more than one class dedicated to improvement;
- ensure all courses align with, and build upon, one another;
- frame courses around improving problems of practice;
- use the practical knowledge of scholarly practitioners and have them apply what they learn in their laboratories of practice;
- have scholarly practitioners implement ideas and collect data along the way;
- encourage cycles of improvement;
- start dissertation work early (on day one) and have scholarly practitioners write their dissertations long the way (note Table 7.1 for an example of this in a three-year program); and
- avoid PhD-lite courses, instead providing rich content geared towards practitioners while expecting quality work.

Re-envision mentoring scholarly practitioners doing ISDiPs

Mentoring in all EdD programs, whether they employ improvement science as a signature methodology or not, should look different than traditional PhD mentoring. Students bring practical expertise that compliments faculty members' content and research expertise. Together, this partnership works to change practice. With the ISDiP, an additional layer of careful mentoring is needed. To this end, programs should mentor students with the understanding that:

- Because performing improvement science is difficult and complex mentoring, developing scholarly practitioners starts from the beginning of the program and continues to the end. In the second year of the program, forming small dissertation support groups allows for peer mentoring support.
- To the extent possible, faculty and program administrators need to be open to new ideas, formats, and processes for the dissertation experience.
- Faculty and administrative processes must be responsive to scholarly practitioners' needs and tolerant of their schedules and obligations. Unexpected turns and unintended consequences are likely to happen along the improvement journey.
- EdD students are professionals who work in complex systems. Faculty should communicate with them openly and honestly and act as a critical friend or thought partner.
- Professionals returning to school need scaffolding and support in their writing. Faculty should teach thinking through writing and set high expectations for all writing.
- Professional preparation should be a decathlon, not a marathon (Shulman, 2010). Faculty should develop ways to measure products and processes to determine student progress and success in the program. They must move away from traditional thinking about rigor (being harsh and rigid) to understanding rigor as leadership in an improvement process (CPED, 2010).

We hope these lessons assist in admissions, teaching, course content, and mentoring. To continue this work, we offer activities and questions based on improvement science that faculty can use to change dissertations to meet the needs of EdD scholarly practitioners.

How to Use the Tools of Improvement Science to Change Dissertations

The above lessons offer basic ideas for changing admissions, courses, teaching and the mentoring of students for ISDiPs. Here, we continue to offer ideas for change using the tools and processes of improvement science. We begin with an overall set of reflective questions about the current state of the dissertations in your program. We then move on to hands-on activities and more reflective questions for you to use to think about and change your dissertations.

Question Set #1

The Current State of Your Dissertations

The purpose of these questions is to help faculty reflect on the current state of their EdD dissertations and consider if they are meeting the needs of working professionals.

1. What are our dissertations like now? What purpose do they serve?
2. What problems/issues do our students focus on? Are these problems focused on the needs of faculty or the needs of students as practitioners? How does literature support the naming and framing of problems?
3. Do students have the opportunity to pose new formats?
4. Do our courses allow students to practice what they learn and build towards the dissertation?
5. What methodologies do we teach? How do they support the dissertation as a means for creating change? Will students use these methodologies after they graduate?
6. What happens to the work once the dissertation is defended?

Activity #1

Creating a Fishbone Diagram

The aim of this activity is to encourage faculty and committee members to collaboratively develop a fishbone diagram aimed at uncovering why traditional dissertations need to change to better meet the needs of EdD students.

A fishbone is a visual tool used to:

- understand a problem *before* interventions are developed (avoids solutionitis);
- discover, organize, and summarize a group's knowledge about the causes contributing to a problem;
- sort causes into useful categories; and
- develop collaboration, facilitate brainstorming, and build consensus.

Step one: Develop a problem statement for the fishbone

Recreate the image in Figure 8.1 on a large piece of chart paper. If the stated problem does not capture a problem that matters to you, alter it. Work to operationally define your problem. Note Figure 8.1, which provides an example.

Step two: Develop categories for your fishbone

Identify one key factor associated with your problem (What is contributing to the problem?). Make this one of the main boxes (categories) on your fishbone. Note Figure 8.2 in which we have placed "faculty lack understanding" as an example category.

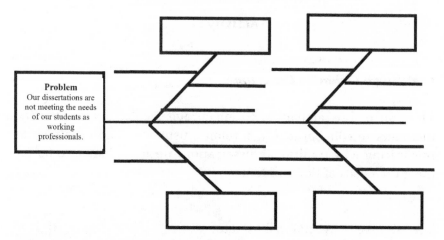

Figure 8.1. Fishbone Problem for Faculty

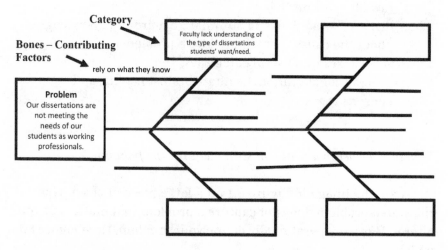

Figure 8.2. Fishbone Categories for Faculty

Step three: Fill in the bones

Fill in the bones above or below your category with contributing factors. For example, a contributing factor as to why faculty lack understanding might be that they rely on what they know/did. Seek factors using the strategy of "five whys," (Serrat, 2009) asking "why" five times as you work (e.g., Why do faculty lack understanding of dissertations aimed at meeting students' needs?). The five whys are helpful when individuals do not truly understand the situation or when a deeper understanding of a complex problem is necessary. The five whys:

- encourage use of higher order thinking skills;
- cut through layers of bureaucracy to find the true meaning;
- challenge perceptions of the current problem;
- reveal root causes to the problem; and
- motivate further digging.

As you work on your fishbone:

- treat all ideas as valid;
- keep an open mind;
- be user-centered;
- avoid jumping to solutions;
- get a variety of perspectives (users, experts, etc.); and
- use available data (where is the "gap?").

Stop when the energy of the group begins to wane.

Questions for discussion

After the fishbone has been completed, use these questions to continue your dialogue.

1. What did we learn about our dissertation from the fishbone? Why are our dissertations not meeting the needs of our students? What factors are contributing to this?
2. What do we think about a fishbone? How might our dissertations benefit if students constructed a fishbone to uncover their PoPs?

Question Set #2

Systems Maps

These questions are aimed at helping faculty and committee members understand the benefits and challenges of systems maps in ISDiPs.

> A systems map is completed after a fishbone. It is an analytic tool that maps essential features of a system that are most likely to manifest themselves as improvement work proceeds. A systems map parses an organization into levels or categories relevant to solving the identified problem.

Questions

1. What systems are hampering us from changing our dissertations? What part of the system do we need to focus on to change our dissertations?
2. What would we need to teach to help students examine their dissertation problems at a systems level? In what course would this be taught?

Activity #2

Developing a Driver Diagram

The purpose of this activity it to provide hands-on experience developing a driver diagram.

> A driver diagram is a tool that visually represents a group's working theory of improvement. A driver diagram creates a common

language and coordinates efforts among different individuals with a common problem. A driver diagram is not intended to communicate the *entire* theory of improvement. It just supplies those parts which are highest leverage. A driver diagram is a "live" document subject to refinement as new learning accumulates. Each driver diagram has these components:

- An Aim Statement
- Primary Drivers
- Secondary Drivers (etc., as needed)
- Change Ideas

Step one: Develop an aim

Recreate the image below on a large piece of chart paper. Then, create an aim statement that is a feasible goal for changing your dissertations. Elements of a powerful aim statement include:

- a clear definition of success for an improvement effort;
- the effort of the change (i.e., the system to improve, the boundaries to set); and
- a clear statement of:
  - how much? (measurable, specific, numerical goals; starting point identified);
  - by when? (time frame); and
  - for what/whom? (target population or setting or system/process).

Note sample aim in Figure 8.3.

Step two: Identify primary and secondary drivers

The first set of underpinning goals are referred to as *primary drivers* because they "drive" the achievement of the aim. These drivers

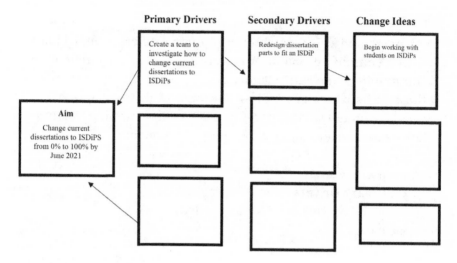

Figure 8.3. Driver Diagram for Faculty

may act independently or in concert to achieve the overall goal.

Identify your primary drivers and place them on your driver diagram.

Secondary drivers activate each primary driver. They are the "how" of change.

Identify your secondary drivers and place them on your driver diagram.

Step three: Develop a change/intervention

The ultimate aim of the driver diagram is to define a set of interventions that can be implemented to achieve the aim. Brainstorm some change ideas for you aim and place them on the right-hand side of your diagram. After you have completed this, use arrows to identify links between your aim, drivers, and change ideas. We have provided samples in Figure 8.3.

Questions for discussion

1. What primary and secondary drivers would we need to focus on to achieve our aim of changing dissertations into ISDiPs?

2. What change idea should we implement first?
3. A driver diagram is a "live" document, subject to refinement. How might our document change as we work on changing our current dissertations into ISDiPs?

Question Set #3

The ISDiP Model of Improvement

These questions are aimed at helping faculty and committee members understand the benefits and challenges of the ISDiP Model of Improvement.

Our Model of Improvement contains four guiding questions and the SIAR cycle (see Chapter 7). Our model structures and guides the improvement process.

Questions for discussion

1. What if we used questions similar to those on the ISDiP Model of Improvement to guide our dissertation redesign process? What if we asked, "What are we trying to improve about our dissertations?" What is the most reasoned change idea for us to try? How will we know if our change was successful? Once we do this, what steps would we need to take next?
2. How might a SIAR cycle help us make change incrementally and, in turn, do a better job?

Question Set #4

Measurement for Improvement

These questions are aimed at helping faculty and committee members understand the distinction between measurement for improvement and what is typically taught in doctoral research courses.

> Measurement for improvement links to the drivers and work processes that are the object of change. Measurement for improvement provides evidence that the intervention is working (or not), for whom, and why.

Questions for discussion

1. Look at Table 8.1 and discuss the similarities and differences you see between data collected for research and data collected for measurement of improvement.
2. Given these differences, how would our research/inquiry courses need to change for ISDiPs?

Table 8.1. Data Collected for Research vs. Measurement for Improvement

Quantitative Research	Qualitative Research	Measurement for Improvement
Purpose: Systematic, empirical, objective investigation of observable phenomena via statistical techniques Theorizes, explains, predicts	**Purpose:** Gathers an in-depth understanding of behavior and the reasons that govern such behavior (micro views) Explores, discovers, is subjective	**Purpose:** Inquiries to improve practice Works toward effectiveness, efficacy, and engagement Accelerates a field's capacity to learn
Data collection aims to understand: Latent variables	**Data collection aims to understand:** Perceptions/lived experiences	**Measures aim to understand:** What worked, for whom, and why • Is the intervention working? (driver measures) • How is it working? (process measures) • Is it working as intended? (balancing measures) • Did it work? (outcome measures)

Quantitative Research	Qualitative Research	Measurement for Improvement
Tools: Tests, closed-ended surveys, etc. Concern for validity and reliability	**Tools:** Protocols, open interviews, open-ended survey items	**Tools:** Gathered in the workplace Fits into the everyday
Qualities of Measures: Numeric Broad and general Structured/formal	**Qualities of Measures:** Words, images, themes, and categories	**Qualities of Measures:** Tied to a working theory of improvement Practical Demonstration of shift in system
Analysis: Sophisticated Trends, comparisons, relationships Objective/unbiased/valid/ reliable Generalizable	**Analysis:** Flexible, emerging, subjective Holistic: identifies patterns, themes Confirmability/ trustworthiness Particularistic	**Analysis:** Continuous: counts, perceptions, ratings, rankings Timely
How data are used: Published in peer-reviewed journals Presented at conferences	**How data are used:** In-depth understanding of viewpoints Published in peer-reviewed journals Presented at conferences	**How findings are used:** Reporting and sharing to stakeholders in practice Building a professional knowledge base

Utilizing Improvement Tools to Overcome Dissertation Challenges for Students

From our work in EdD programs, we understand that working professionals want their dissertations to have an impact on their contexts and themselves as leaders. However, we also realize that they sacrifice personally and professionally when undertaking a three-year degree process. Earning an EdD requires motivation, resources, and much support. According to a 2004 study by the Council of Graduate Schools, mental burn out is the number one reason doctoral students (EdDs and PhDs) leave their programs. Such burnout happens at two points in doctoral preparation. The first point is during the initial two years, when the heavy demands of doctoral work are first experienced. The second point is after all coursework is completed, when the isolation of dissertation work begins. While data is limited on persistence of EdD students, we reviewed the graduate profiles on CPED's website to gain insight as to why these individuals persisted and completed their programs. In these profiles, students gave reasons such as:

- being able to apply what they learned to their contexts;
- learning to become a consumer of educational research while subsequently learning how to utilize research to change what they do;
- improving and expanding their thinking, research skills, professionalism, and ability to synthesize information;
- having a good mentor and the support of a cohort, especially during dissertation time;
- connecting with professors, committee members, and peers passionate about educational improvement; and
- having professors who value life in schools and who value their time.

So, how did these successful graduates do it? How did they overcome the challenges of working full-time while completing a DiP? Why was doing a DiP so important to them? The next activities using the tools of improvement science can be used to answer questions like these.

Activity #1

Creating a Fishbone Diagram

The purpose of developing a fishbone diagram is to reveal some of the challenges scholarly practitioners may face (or are facing) completing an ISDiP. This activity provides a hands-on experience with an improvement tool.

A fishbone is a:

- visual means to understand a problem before interventions are developed (avoid solutionitis);
- visual tool for discovering, organizing, and summarizing knowledge about the causes contributing to a problem;
- tool to sort causes into useful categories; and
- tool used to develop collaboration, facilitate brainstorming, and consensus.

Step one: Develop a problem statement for your fishbone

Recreate the image in Figure 8.4 on a large piece of chart paper. If this problem does not fit, write your own problem statement.

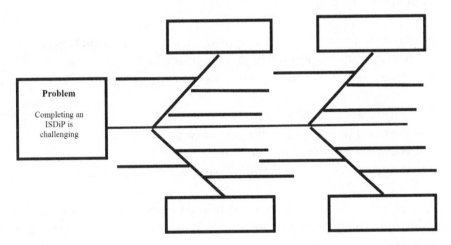

Figure 8.4. Fishbone Problem for Students

Step two: Develop categories on your fishbone

Identify one key factor associated with your problem (What is contributing to your problem?). Make this one of the main boxes (categories) on your fishbone. In the sample, we have placed four examples in Figure 8.5.

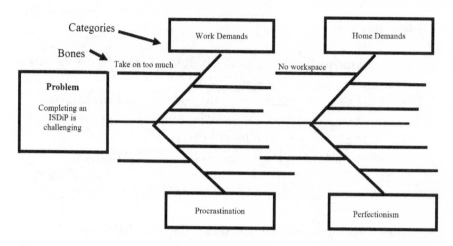

Figure 8.5. Fishbone Categories for Students

Step three: Fill in the bones

Fill in the bones of your category with contributing factors. We have written in a few examples in the diagram. As you work ask "why" five times. Below are some examples of how you can ask "why":

- Why is work so demanding?
- Why do I procrastinate writing each day?
- Why do I feel overwhelmed?
- Why do I keep writing and revising the same sentence?

As you work, remember you are brainstorming. Treat all ideas as valid and avoid jumping to solutions. Stop when your energy begins to wane.

Show your fishbone to others

Once you have completed your fishbone, share it with other students, family members, or work colleagues who understand your challenges. Ask them if you have defined your problem. When appropriate, modify your fishbone based on their input.

Questions for discussions

1. What insights about completing an ISDiP did you gain from your fishbone?
2. What was it like sharing your fishbone with others? Did their input provide more information?

Activity #1

Developing a Driver Diagram

The purpose of this activity it to provide a hands-on experience developing a personal driver diagram.

A driver diagram is a tool that visually represents a working theory of improvement. A driver diagram is not intended to communicate your *entire* theory, just those parts which are highest leverage in achieving your goal. A driver diagram is a "live" document, subject to refinement as new learning accumulates and changes ideas. Each driver diagram has these components:

- Aim
- Primary Drivers
- Secondary Drivers (etc., as needed)
- Change Ideas

Step one: Develop an aim

Recreate the image in Figure 8.7 on a large piece of chart paper. Then, use your fishbone to create an aim statement. Elements of a powerful aim include:

- a clear definition of success for an improvement effort;
- the effort of the change (i.e., the system to improve, the boundaries to set); and

- a clear statement of:
  - how much? (measureable, specific, numerical goals; starting point identified);
  - by when? (time frame); and
  - for what/whom? (target population or setting or system/process).

Figure 8.6 contains an example aim statement in the box on the left side.

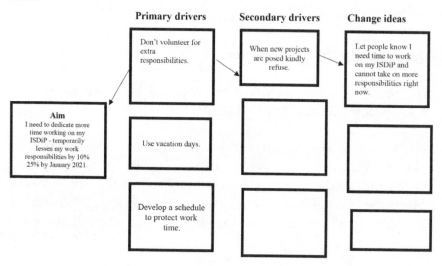

Figure 8.6. Driver Diagram for Students

The Habits of a Scholarly Practitioner

To end this chapter, we return to the habits of an improver we discussed in Chapter 1, developed by Lucas and Nacer (2015). We believe habits are key because they define the ways of doing and being as a professional in a certain field. The field of education, like healthcare, needs individuals who have strong habits that drive them to improve the contexts they serve. Like Lucas and Nacer (2015), we advocate for improvement science as the signature methodology to develop the habits of an improver in EdD programs. Therefore, if improvement science is going to be a frame for dissertations in EdD programs, then faculty need to identify and articulate how the improvers in our field think, act, and feel and what they need to be able to know and do. That is, we need to articulate the habitual knowledge, skills, and dispositions effective improvers in education need.

Wood (2007) defines a habit as a routine set of behaviors that occur subconsciously and regularly. There are three types of habits: motor (movement), intellectual (perception, logic, reasoning), and character (trust, ethics, responsibility). A habit becomes a fixed way of thinking, willing, or feeling when a behavior is repeated over and over again. To develop a new habit, one must create a specific and reasonable goal, commit to that goal, repeatedly take baby steps towards it, and loop in other people who can help them achieve it. Repetition is the key to starting a habit. But eventually, one must go from simply *doing the behavior* to making the behavior a core part of one's identity. Clear (2018) calls changing a behavior an identity-based habit, one that has become so ingrained and natural that it reflects who one is on the inside. Identity-based habits make each of us unique because they show the world the type of person we desire to be (our core principles and values). To develop identity-based habits, one must practice (apply what is learned), use their intellect (perception, logic, reasoning) and enact good character (be trustworthy, ethical, responsible). Blending understanding habits with CPED's definition of a scholarly practitioner offers EdD faculty and students the habits educational improvers need. The habits of a scholarly practitioner are captured in Figure 8.7.

Knowledge: Intellectual Habits

Scholarly practitioners are working professionals who, by nature and experience, want to improve their contexts. Scholarly practitioners believe all students can learn, and they work to make this belief a reality by applying their knowledge to their practice (Moore, 2017; Bryk, 2018). To do this, scholarly practitioners habitually ask questions, work on improving problems, and engage with literature to find answers. We elaborate on each of these habits next.

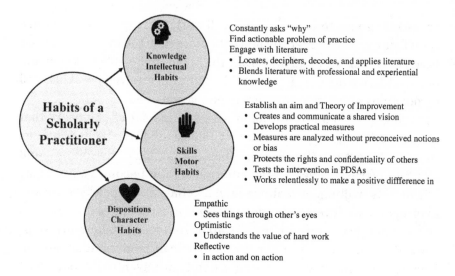

Figure 8.7. Habits of a Scholarly Practitioner

Question

Curiosity is central to improvement, and educational improvers habitually ask, "What problem of practice needs to be addressed to make my context more equitable, ethical, and just?"

Find actionable problems of practice

When questions are asked, issues and problems arise. Scholarly practitioners habitually use the tools and processes of improvement science (e.g., fishbones, systems maps) to uncover the nature of the problems they see.

Engage with literature

Scholarly practitioners know the problems they face are messy and complex, and they understand that they alone do not have all the answers. Given this, they habitually turn to literature and other experts in the field. They locate, decipher, decode, and apply literature to design interventions.

Scholarly practitioners habitually turn to literature but, because of their vast practical experience, they read analytically, carefully considering how the information they read applies to their contexts. Habitually engaging with literature expands a scholarly practitioner's knowledge base as well as their logic and reasoning skills

Skills: Motor Habits

When problems become evident, scholarly practitioners do not sit on the sidelines. They develop an aim, create a theory of improvement, implement it, and measure its effects. Thinking and acting like this become habits of leadership. We elaborate on these next.

Establish an aim and theory of improvement

When action is necessary, scholarly practitioners habitually use the tools of improvement science. They work with others to create a diver diagram that contains an aim and working theory of improvement. Scholarly practitioners are habitually goal centered, facilitative, or user centered. They take time to listen to the concerns of others and use what they hear to make decisions, balancing possibilities with unintended consequences. Scholarly practitioners are cautious but bold. They understand that when it comes to leading schools and organizations, not taking a risk can be a greater risk than taking one. Scholarly practitioners set aims but are flexible. They see setbacks as part of the growth process (Moore, 2017).

Develop practical measures

Given today's world of accountability, educators know they must prove their effectiveness. Scholarly practitioners do this habitually. They collect baseline data prior to implementing an intervention and collect more once improvement efforts begin. Scholarly practitioners habitually develop and use a range of practical measures and analyze the data they collect without preconceptions or bias. Visuals and stories are habitually used to communicate their findings.

Test the theory/intervention

Scholarly practitioners learn by doing, and, because of this, they understand the value of cycles of improvement. Scholarly practitioners understand that complex PoPs are solved incrementally, not quickly or easily. Given this, they are patient and collaborative. They habitually work side-by-side alongside others and, in doing so, see possibilities. They habitually ask, "What if ... ?" (Lucas & Nacer, 2015).

Dispositions: Character Habits

Improving anything is almost always a social endeavor, requiring buy-in and engagement from others. To accomplish this, scholarly practitioners need professional dispositions, or values, commitments, and ethics (Shulman, 1986), dispositions that lead to open-mindedness and reflectivity. Scholarly practitioners habitually approach their work with presence and awareness of others' thoughts and feelings (Ennis, 2002, 2004).

Empathic

To influence individuals in their contexts, scholarly practitioners must understand them. An essential part of understanding is the ability to "read" individuals. Scholarly practitioners accomplish this by habitually questioning how others feel and what they are thinking. Scholarly practitioners are in tune to every person and every conversation regardless of the message (Moore, 2017). Being habitually empathic requires scholarly practitioners to see things through others' eyes and walk in their shoes.

Optimistic

Anchor (2011) notes that happiness does not stem from the belief that we do not need to change, but from realization that we can. Happiness and optimism go hand and hand and are the precursors to success. Scholarly practitioners habitually remain optimistic.

They detach from events (do not take them personally), see setbacks as temporary (not permanent), and set boundaries (do not allow criticism to infiltrate their self-worth). Scholarly practitioners are not overly optimistic. They understand improvement comes from effort and hard work.

Reflective

Scholarly practitioners are reflective leaders who constantly ask themselves questions. Schön (1984) calls this type of behavior reflection-in-action and reflection-on-action. Reflection-in-action occurs when a professional takes action on an unfamiliar situation using their past experience and knowledge. A scholarly practitioner who reflects-in-action "is not dependent on the categories of established theory and technique but constructs a new theory of the unique case" (Schön 1984, p. 68). Blending scholarship with one's professional knowledge to understand a problem is an example of reflection-in-action. Scholarly practitioners habitually reflect-in-action but they also reflect-*on*-the actions they take. After they implement an intervention, they habitually and frequently ask themselves questions like:

- What happened as a result of leadership?
- What are my reactions and feelings to what others say?
- Did I respect the inherent dignity and worth of each individual?
- Did I model respect for diverse community stakeholders and treat them equitably?
- Was I constantly assessing my own personal assumptions, values, beliefs, and practices?
- Did I respectfully challenge and work to change assumptions and beliefs that negatively impact others?

Questions like these become habitual for scholarly practitioners.

Summary

This chapter continued the conversation on ISDiPs by exposing challenges faculty and mentors may face when they attempt to change an entrenched tradition like the dissertation. To assist in moving ideas forward, we provided insight into out lessons learned, hands-on activities that use the tools of improvement and reflective questions. For scholarly practitioners, this chapter contained two hands-on activities using the tools of improvement science to help scholarly practitioners understand the challenges they may face when writing their dissertation. The chapter ended with our vision of the habits of a scholarly practitioner doing improvement work.

Post-reading questions for faculty

1. What did you think about Nick Sousanis's dissertation? What would it take to get faculty like yourself to think about the dissertation in new and different ways?
2. Looking at the lessons learned, discuss which ones seem most feasible for you right now?
3. What did you learn about revising your dissertations from the hands-on activities and questions?

Post-reading questions for scholarly practitioners/students

1. What insights did you gain using the tools of improvement science?
2. Can you think of any other habits that could be added to Figure 8.1? Explain what they would be and the benefits they would bring.

References

Anchor, S. (2011). The happiness advantage: The seven principles that fuel success and performance at work. Virgin Publishing, London, UK.

Bryk, A.S. (2018, April 3). *Advancing quality in continuous improvement.* Speech presented at the Carnegie Foundation Summit on Improvement in Education, San Francisco, CA.

Bryk, A.S., Gomez, L.M., Gunrow, A., & LeMahieu, P.G. (2015). Breaking the cycle of failed school reforms: Using network improvement communities to learn fast and implement well. *Harvard Education Letter,* *31*(1), 1–3.

Carnegie Project for the Educational Doctorate (CPED). (2010). *Design concept definitions.* Retrieved from https://cped.memberclicks.net/the-framework

Clear, J. (2018) *Atomic habits: An easy & proven way to build good habits and break bad ones.* Avery, NY.

Council of Graduate Schools (2004). PhD completion and attrition: Policies, numbers leadership and next steps. Council of Graduate Schools, Washington, D.C.

Dunn, S, (2014). The amazing adventures of the comic book dissertator. Retrieved 29 December 2019 from, *The Chronicle of Higher Education.* https://chroniclevitae.com/news/361-the-amazing-adventures-of-the-comic-book-dissertator

Ennis, R.H. (2002). Goals for a critical thinking curriculum and its assessment. In A. L. Costa (Ed.), *Developing minds (3rd Edition).* Alexandria, VA: ASCD, 44–46.

Ennis, R.H. (2004). Applying soundness standards to qualified reasoning. *Informal Logic, 24*(1), 23–39.

Erickson, F., & Gutiérrez, K. (2002). Comment: Culture, rigor, and science in educational research. *Educational Researcher, 3*(8), pp. 21–24.

Gutiérrez, K.D. & Penuel, W.R. (2014). Relevance to practice as a criterion for rigor. *Educational Researcher, 43*(1). pp. 19–23.

Gutiérrez, K.D. & Vossoughi, S. (2010). Lifting off the ground to return anew: Mediated praxis, transformative learning, and social design experiments. *Journal of Teacher Education, 61*(1–2). p. 100–117.

Kennedy, B.L., Altman, M., & Pizano, A. (2018). Engaging in the battle of the snails by challenging the traditional dissertation model. *Impacting Education, 3*(1), 1–12.

Lucas, B. & Nacer, H. (2015). *The habits of an improver: Thinking about learning for improvement in health care.* London: Health Foundation.

Moore, B. (2017, July 7). Mindsets, dispositions and practices of highly effective school leaders. [Blog post]. *Epic Impact Education Group*. Retrieved from: https://www.epicimpactedgroup.com/blog/2017/7/7/mindsets-dispositions-and-practices-of-highly-effective-school-leaders

Patton, S. (2013). The dissertation can no longer be defended. *Chronicle of Higher Education*, available at http://chronicle.com/article/The-Dissertation-Can-No-Longer/137215

Perry, J.A. (2014). Changing schools of education through grassroots faculty-led change. *Innovative Higher Education, 39*(2), Pp. 155–168.

Ravitch, S.M. & Lytle, S.L. (2016). Becoming practitioner-scholars: The role of practice-based inquiry dissertations in the development of educational leaders. In V.A. Storey and K.A. Hesbol (Eds.) *Contemporary approaches to dissertation development and research methods*. IGI Global, Hershey, PA.

Schön, D.A. (1984). The reflective practitioner: How professionals think in action. Basic Books, Inc. NY.

Schuster, J., & Finkelstein, M. (2006). *The American faculty: The restructuring of academic work and careers*. Baltimore, MD: Johns Hopkins Press.

Serrat, O. (2009). The five whys of technique. *Knowledge Solutions*, Springer, Singapore.

Shulman, L.S. (1986). Those who understand: Knowledge growth in teaching. *Educational Researcher, 15*(2), pp. 4–14.

Shulman, L.S. (2010). Doctoral Education shouldn't be a marathon the salvation may mean embracing the enemy: Professional schools. Retrieved 10 November 2019 from, *The Chronical of Higher Education*, https://www.chronicle.com/article/Doctoral-Education-Isnt-a/64883.

Sousanis, N., (2015). *Unflattening*. Harvard University Press, Cambridge, MA.

Sousanis, N., (2014). *Unflattening: A visual-verbal inquiry into learning in many dimensions*. (Unpublished doctoral dissertation). Teachers College, Columbia University.

Thomson, E.A., Auhl, G., Hicks, K., McPherson, K., Robinson, C., & Wood, D. (2017). Course design as a collaborative enterprise: Incorporating interdisciplinarity into a backward mapping systems approach to course design in higher education. In R. Walker, & S. Bedford (Eds.), *Research and development in higher education: Curriculum transformation volume 40: Refereed papers from the 40th HERDSA Annual International Conference* (pp. 356-367). [Paper 85] Sydney, NSW: Higher Education Research and Development Society of Australasia.

Tierney, W.G. (1998). Organizational culture in higher education: Defining the essentials. *The Journal of Higher Education, 59*(1), pp. 2-21.

Valenti, R., & Inman, D. (2010). *Completing a professional practice dissertation: A guide for doctoral students and faculty.* Charlotte, NC: Information Age Publishing.

Wood, W. & Neal, D.T. (2007). *A new look at habits and the habit-goal interface. Psychological Review, 114*(4): 843-863.

ABOUT THE AUTHORS

Jill Perry, PhD is the Executive Director of the Carnegie Project on the Education Doctorate (CPED) and an Associate Professor of Practice in the Department of Educational Foundations, Organizations, and Policy at the University of Pittsburgh. Her research focuses on professional doctorate preparation in education, organizational change in higher education, and faculty leadership roles. Her publications have appeared in *Planning and Changing Journal, Journal of School Public Relations, Innovation in Higher Education,* and in several books and practitioner journals. She has edited two books and is currently researching the ways EdD programs teach practitioners to utilize research evidence. Dr. Perry received a PhD in International Education Policy from the University of Maryland. She also received a master's degree in Higher Education Administration and a bachelor's degree in Spanish and International Studies from Boston College. She has over 20 years of experience in leadership and program development in education and teaching experience at the elementary, secondary, undergraduate, and graduate levels in the United States and abroad. She is a Fulbright Scholar (Germany) and a returned Peace Corps volunteer (Paraguay).

Debby Zambo, PhD is an Associate Professor Emerita from Arizona State University currently working as the Associate Director of CPED. Debby has been involved with improvement science, CPED, and the Carnegie Foundation since their early Explorer's Workshops in 2015. Since then, she has been a member and cofounder of CPED's Improvement Science Interest Group and a member of the Carnegie Foundation's Higher Education Network. Debby has also made presentations on improvement science at CPED Convenings and the Carnegie Foundation Summit. With Jill Perry and Robert Crow, she developed and presented five workshops on a range of topics, including the basic tools and processes of improvement science, deeper philosophical ideals and complexities, and most recently, contextualizing improvement science in dissertation work.

Robert Crow, PhD is an Associate Professor of Educational Research at West Carolina University's (WCU's) College of Education and Allied Professions. Dr. Crow previously served as Coordinator of Instructional Development & Assessment for WCU's Coulter Faculty Commons, working primarily in faculty professional development. Dr. Crow's expertise in assessment and evaluation has led to collaborations with other 4-year institutions, community colleges, PK-12 schools, and institutional accreditation agencies such as Southern Association of Colleges and Schools Commission on Colleges (SACSCOC). Dr. Crow's research interests include improvement science and assessment and evaluation of student learning and development. He is the co-editor of the recent publication, *The Educational Leader's Guide to Improvement Science: Data, Design and Cases for Reflection* (2019). Dr. Crow currently co-leads the CPED Improvement Group (CIG) for Improvement Science with Debby Zambo and is a Carnegie national faculty member for networked improvement science.

INDEX